ndolph B.
never in

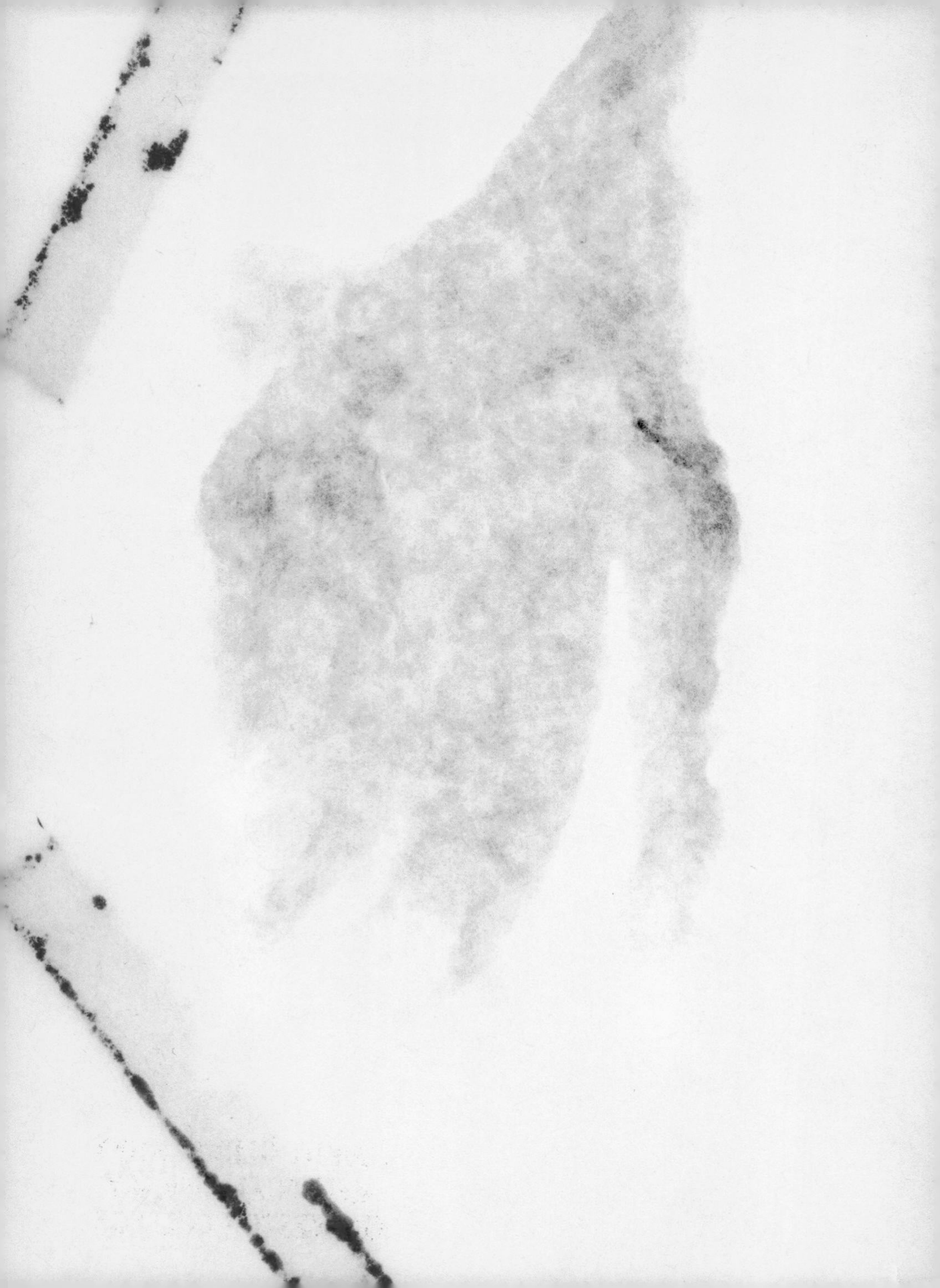

Wealth and Power in Antebellum Texas

Wealth and Power in Antebellum Texas

By

Randolph B. Campbell

AND

Richard G. Lowe

Texas A&M University Press

COLLEGE STATION AND LONDON

Library of Congress Cataloging in Publication Data

Campbell, Randolph B 1940-
Wealth and power in antebellum Texas.

Bibliography: p.
Includes index.
1. Wealth — Texas — History. I. Lowe, Richard G., 1942- joint author. II. Title.
HC107.T43W43 330.9′764′04 76-51652
ISBN 0-89096-030-5

Manufactured in the United States of America
FIRST EDITION

Contents

List of Tables

List of Figures

Preface

AMERICANS have long lived with an optimistic view of their society that may be termed the "egalitarian ideal." Although concentrated wealth and undemocratic politics have not always been ignored, the American past has usually been seen in terms of relative economic equality and political democracy. There is, however, always the problem of the antebellum South with its "peculiar institution" of Negro slavery. It has stood in general as the most likely exception to the egalitarian ideal of the American people.

How closely did the antebellum South approximate the popular ideal of economic equality and political democracy? The answer to this question can reveal much concerning the distribution of wealth and power in Southern society, and this alone is extremely important for an understanding of pre-Civil War America. But another question follows: if the South did indeed diverge from the ideal, was it therefore greatly different from the rest of the United States? Perhaps for the nation as a whole the egalitarian ideal was more myth than reality.

How did the South compare with the rest of the United States in terms of economic and political arrangements? If circumstances in the South did not approximate those in the free states, this may be taken as further evidence that the historical experience of Southerners, as some scholars have suggested, differs significantly from that of other Americans. If, on the other hand, circumstances were very similar in both sections, historians must look elsewhere in order to explain the South's distinctiveness. And they must also ask how closely the entire nation, not just the South, conformed to the egalitarian ideal.

The purpose of this study is to investigate these questions through an analysis of wealth and power in antebellum Texas. Obviously, many aspects of such an investigation demand a quantitative approach. "Wealth" by definition is a matter of numbers, a combination of real and personal property values. But "power," although partly susceptible to quantitative analysis, can never be conclusively measured simply in terms of numbers. Thus, we have combined quantitative methods with more traditional historical research to study all important facets of the egalitarian ideal in antebellum Texas.

Before we outline our specific approach to this problem, there is one word of caution the reader should keep in mind. In general, the egalitarian ideal is seen in a positive light, as a "good" thing for a democratic society. The attainment of this ideal, however, is almost certainly impossible for any length of time. Men are not equal in intelligence, ambition, and character. And even if they were, older men have had more time to accumulate wealth than have younger men; so inequality arises. Moreover, the attainment of this ideal would doubtless have some negative implications for a capitalist economic system. Could there, for example, be the necessary accumulation of investment capital in a society marked by absolute equality of wealth? Thus, the egalitarian ideal is and must be unattainable in absolute terms. In general, we present the ideal in positive terms, primarily because it is popularly regarded as a "good thing," but we recognize that some inequality is probably necessary and inevitable. The question is, how close did antebellum Texas come to the ideal, and how did the wealthholding situation in Texas compare with those in other places and other times?

Chapter 1 provides a detailed historiographical context for an investigation of the distribution of wealth and power in the antebellum South. This chapter also reduces general areas of analysis to a number of very precise, explicit questions. The second chapter briefly describes Texas in the 1850's in the traditional historical manner and outlines our quantitative methodology. Chapters 3 and 4 analyze wealthholding and the characteristics of wealthholders in the Lone Star state. The following chapters (5 and 6) focus more narrowly on the distribution of agricultural property and production and on wealthholding in Texas towns in 1850 and 1860. Chapter 7 juxtaposes the economic status of political leaders with that of the sample population. The final chapter compares wealthholding circumstances in Texas with conditions in other areas of the antebellum

United States and with wealthholding arrangements in the nation a century later.

In writing these chapters we have sought to employ those statistical tools necessary for full and accurate quantitative analysis. At the same time we have attempted to explain those statistical tools we did use in clear and simple language. We hope that the overall result will satisfy and be useful to both quantitative and more traditional historians.

In the research and writing of this book we have received aid from numerous individuals. Professor Leo Estrada of the sociology department at North Texas State University provided invaluable assistance in developing appropriate quantitative research methods. The county map of antebellum Texas was drawn by Professor Terry G. Jordan of the geography department. John Heffley also gave us his professional help in the preparation of maps, charts, and tables for the book. Steve Minnis of the computing center at North Texas constantly advised us on the handling of our data and wrote several special computer programs for our project. Steve is at least as efficient as the IBM computer itself. Professor Robert Gallman of the economics department at the University of North Carolina read the entire manuscript and suggested many needed corrections. Our colleague in the history department, Donald Chipman, also provided a valuable reading of the manuscript. Any remaining mistakes in the book, of course, are our responsibility.

The collection of data was handled speedily and efficiently by a number of our students at North Texas: Theresa Haynie, Rex Hiatt, Susan Rakow, Beverly Ritchie, Maury Fortin, and Ruth Sheehan. Expert typing of the text and tables was done by Paula House and Denise Infante. Throughout the years of research and writing the Committee on Faculty Research at North Texas State University provided generous financial assistance for this project.

Chapter 7 of this book appeared in a slightly different form as an article in the July, 1975, number of the *Southwestern Historical Quarterly*. Appendix 2 first appeared in the *Journal of American History* (September, 1976). We wish to thank these two journals for their permission to publish this material in fuller context.

Wealth and Power in Antebellum Texas

Chapter 1.

Introduction

THERE is a long-standing disagreement among historians concerning a question basic to the interpretation of antebellum Southern society. Was the Old South a land of relative economic equality and political democracy for its free population, or was it a section marked by great inequality in the distribution of wealth and dominated politically as well as economically by an elite slaveholding aristocracy? Perhaps the question poses an oversimplified dichotomy, especially in asking if politics was aristocratic or democratic, but the historical debate has given it this general form at present.

The modern historiography of this question began primarily with the work of Ulrich B. Phillips. Writing in the early twentieth century, Phillips emphasized the tendency of the "plantation regime" to replace smaller farmers in most of the staple-producing areas of the Old South. Planters holding large numbers of slaves came to own most of the best land and pushed smaller farmers, especially non-slaveholders, onto inferior land and into a subordinate position. Lewis C. Gray, in his monumental *History of Agriculture in the Southern United States to 1860*, published in 1933, agreed with Phillips' planter-dominance thesis. While arguing that the plantation system eventually tended to decline in old planting regions, Gray emphasized the "prior tendency" of the slave system to destroy the free yeoman who depended on small farming. Neither Phillips nor Gray gave much attention to political arrangements, but the implications of their argument seem clear — planters ruled the wealth-producing and therefore most influential areas of the Old South.[1]

The planter-dominance thesis was never accepted without question by all Southern historians, and in the 1940's it was seriously challenged by Frank L. Owsley and his students from Vanderbilt University. The Owsley school, basing their research on Alabama, Mississippi, Louisiana, and Tennessee, insisted that too great an emphasis on the slaveholding planters had created an incorrect view of antebellum society. They countered with evidence that there was a large middle class who operated "typical" Southern farms, that these yeoman farmers (who were often non-slaveholders) owned their fair share of land comparable in quality with that worked by planters, and that this class of smaller farmers actually prospered and expanded during the 1850's. Owsley also insisted that political arrangements in the Old South were essentially democratic. Even if the planter class occupied the elective offices and determined governmental policy (a fact of which he was not certain), this was due, Owsley said, to "the respect the plain folk of a community had for the character and judgment of individual planters in that community and such qualities of character and judgment in the planter were revealed only by his genuine participation in community affairs." In other words, any political influence enjoyed by the aristocracy was fairly earned and democratically gained.[2]

[1]Ulrich B. Phillips, *American Negro Slavery: A Survey of the Supply, Employment, and Control of Negro Labor as Determined by the Plantation Regime*, p. 336; *idem*, "The Origin and Growth of the Southern Black Belts," *American Historical Review* 11 (July, 1906), 798-816; Lewis Cecil Gray, *History of Agriculture in the Southern United States to 1860*, I, 444-445, 532-537.

[2]Frank L. Owsley and Harriet C. Owsley, "The Economic Basis of Society in the Late Ante-Bellum South," *Journal of Southern History* 6 (February, 1940), 24-25; for the quotation, see Frank Lawrence Owsley, *Plain Folk of the Old South*, pp. 138-139. Two examples of the work of the Owsley school are Herbert Weaver, *Mississippi Farmers, 1850-1860*, and Blanche H. Clark, *The Tennessee Yeoman, 1840-1860*. A statement of the yeoman-democracy thesis that preceded the planter-dominance view is Gustavus W. Dyer, *Democracy in the South before the Civil War*.

An important critique of the Owsley yeoman-democracy thesis by Fabian Linden appeared in the *Journal of Negro History* in 1946. Linden generally accepted the Owsley school's evidence concerning the existence of a large class of small and medium farmers, but he pointed out that the mere existence of these farmers did not prove that they were participating on an equal footing, economically or politically, with the large planters. It would be more revealing, Linden contended, to determine the relative shares of Southern agricultural wealth and production controlled by the planters and yeoman farmers respectively. Linden also made other damaging criticisms of the data, methods, and conclusions of the Owsley-school studies. He pointed out, for example, that an increase from 1850 to 1860 in the percentage of the farm population owning land did not necessarily prove that there was an expansion of farm ownership in favor of smaller farmers. In some counties the higher percentage resulted from a decrease in the number of farmers rather than an increase in landholding, a situation suggesting that small farmers were sometimes "on the move" rather than "on the make" as Owsley had claimed.[3]

Owsley replied to Linden's criticisms in 1947 and in 1949 published his main work in this area, *Plain Folk of the Old South*, but historians did not pursue the question. With the exception of Eugene Genovese's celebrated reformulation of the planter-dominance thesis into an interpretation of the Old South as a precapitalist society, there was little further study of these conflicting interpretations during the next twenty years. Then in 1970 an article in *Agricultural History* by Gavin Wright, an economist, reopened the debate in a limited way.[4]

[3]Fabian Linden, "Economic Democracy in the Slave South: An Appraisal of Some Recent Views," *Journal of Negro History* 31 (April, 1946), 140-190.

[4]Frank L. Owsley, "Communications to the Editor," *American Historical Review* 52 (July, 1947), 845-849; Eugene D. Genovese, *The Political Economy of Slavery: Studies in the Economy and Society of the Slave South;* Gavin Wright, " 'Economic Democracy' and the Concentration of Agricultural Wealth in the Cotton South, 1850-1860," *Agricultural History* 44 (January, 1970), 63-93.

Wright examined the distribution of agricultural wealth in the Cotton South on the basis of an extensive sample of farm operators drawn from the United States census returns for 1850 and 1860 and provided new quantitative evidence to support the Phillips-Gray view of Southern society. His study demonstrated a significantly high degree of concentration of Southern agricultural property and production in the hands of wealthy planters, but it did not attempt to deal thoroughly with all aspects of the planter-dominance versus yeoman-democracy question. The sample from the census returns of 1850 and 1860 on which Wright based his work included only farm operators in large cotton-growing counties, and he did not distinguish between slaveholding and non-slaveholding farmers. Thus his study did not examine changes in the percentage of landholding and landless farmers, and it did not compare the relative positions of slaveholding and non-slaveholding farmers (two of Owsley's main concerns). Wright proceeded primarily by using the Lorenz curve and Gini index to measure the degree of concentration in improved farm acreage, farm value, slave property, cotton production, and agricultural wealth and by examining the relative shares of these categories of farm property held by the richest 5 percent and the poorest 50 percent of farm operators. This approach tended to draw attention to the wealthier classes, and it did not allow him to indicate in detail the changes taking place in the relative positions of small, medium, and large farmers during the 1850's. Finally, Wright treated the question purely as a matter of economic consideration and made no attempt to relate the inequalities in agricultural wealthholding to possible political domination by large planters.[5]

In summary, then, the basic question concerning the distribution of wealth and power in antebellum Southern society remains remarkably open. Owsley and his disciples demonstrated that the planter-dominance thesis amounted in many ways to an oversimplified version of Southern society — enslaved blacks and impoverished whites ruled by an aristocracy of elite planters — not unlike the view held by nineteenth-century

[5]Wright, "'Economic Democracy' and Agricultural Wealth," pp. 63-93.

anti-Southern writers.[6] Linden and Wright in turn argued convincingly that the methods and statistics of the Owsley school did not properly recognize and present the degree of concentration of agricultural wealth in the Old South.

One limitation of all these works is their focus on the farm population alone. Although farmers were clearly the single largest economic group in the Southern population, a sizable proportion of the Old South's people were engaged in pursuits other than agriculture. As Gavin Wright pointed out in his 1970 article, a definitive study of this question would examine the wealth distributions for the *entire* free population, not just farmers alone.[7] But historians have yet to employ both quantitative and traditional methods of research to study intensively the distributions of wealth and the interplay of economic and political relationships among the entire free population of the antebellum South.

The need for such investigation has been generally recognized in recent years. In 1967 David M. Potter pointed to the question of economic classes and political power in the antebellum period as one of the fundamental challenges facing students of Southern history. Reviewing recent works on the cotton economy in 1970, Morton Rothstein concluded that "there is still uncertainty as to whether they [large slaveholders] dominated the cotton frontier in any sense: political, economic or social," and called for "more careful analysis of the structure of ownership" and "the attendant issues raised by Frank Owsley and Fabian Linden and reformulated in the work of Eugene Genovese." John R. Howe, in his recent study of American society in the early nineteenth century,

[6]Frederick Law Olmsted is the most widely read and frequently cited anti-Southern writer of the antebellum period. Virtually every history of Southern social and economic life relies to some extent on his three traveler's accounts: *A Journey in the Seaboard Slave States, with Remarks on Their Economy; A Journey Through Texas: or, A Saddle-Trip on the Southwestern Frontier, with a Statistical Appendix;* and *A Journey in the Back Country.*

[7]Wright, " 'Economic Democracy' and Agricultural Wealth," p. 69.

commented that "aside from Genovese's work, Southern social structure is badly in need of fresh appraisals."[8]

Thus, the need for further analysis of the questions discussed by Phillips, Gray, Owsley, Linden, and Wright is evident; this study of Texas in the 1850's represents an effort to meet it in part. New investigations of old questions must necessarily build on previous work, but they should also offer an improved methodology and be based on more complete data subjected to more rigorous analysis. We believe that a combination of computer-aided quantitative methods with more traditional historical research to study the whole free population as well as farm operators meets the requirements for an essentially new approach. Furthermore, this study, because it deals with Texas, offers several additional possibilities for fresh insight into antebellum Southern society. The Lone Star state is beyond the geographical area covered by the published work of the Owsley school, but it was a very important part of the cotton frontier of the 1850's. An investigation of the distribution of wealth and power in Texas brings into focus a hitherto unexamined area and provides information on economic classes and political arrangements in a relatively young and rapidly developing part of the slave South. In addition, the new southwest was generally recognized as holding the future of the Cotton Kingdom in the 1850's, and developments there took on great significance for all of the antebellum South.

The general question posed by the modern historiography of antebellum Southern economic class structure and political power arrangements should now be clear. To repeat: was the Old South a land of relative economic equality and political democracy for its free population, or was it a section marked by great inequality in the distribution of wealth and

[8]David M. Potter, "Depletion and Renewal in Southern History," in Edgar T. Thompson, ed., *Perspectives on the South: Agenda for Research*, pp. 84-85; Morton Rothstein, "The Cotton Frontier of the Antebellum United States: A Methodological Battleground," *Agricultural History* 44 (January, 1970), 159-160; John R. Howe, *From the Revolution through the Age of Jackson: Innocence and Empire in the Young Republic*, p. 210.

dominated politically as well as economically by an elite slaveholding aristocracy? In limiting the question to Texas in the 1850's, this study will focus on a number of more precise questions that must be made explicit at this point.

What was the degree of equality or inequality in the distribution of wealth among the entire free population of Texas in 1850 and in 1860? This is still a large question, and its answer depends on a careful definition of the term *wealth* and on the use of precise and systematic measurements. But once the necessary definitions and statistical tools are utilized, the extent of economic equality or inequality can be measured with precision. This question also demands an understanding of the relative positions of large, medium, and small wealthholders. And it calls for special attention to the direction and degree of change in the concentration of wealth in Texas from 1850 to 1860.

Once the degree of concentration in wealthholding has been demonstrated, questions remain concerning the characteristics of individual wealthholders. How did age, birthplace, and occupation affect wealthholding? What distinguished the large (richest), middle, and small (poorest) wealthholding classes? What were the comparative economic circumstances of the slaveholding and non-slaveholding segments of the population?

What was the degree of equality or inequality in the distribution of agricultural property and production among the farming population of Texas in 1850 and in 1860? This question calls for an examination of the relative positions of planters and medium and small farmers, and a comparison of the agricultural holdings of slaveholding as opposed to non-slaveholding farmers. Finally, what was the direction and degree of change in the concentration of agricultural property and production from 1850 to 1860? Did the position of the small farmers and non-slaveholders become stronger or weaker relative to that of planters and slaveholders? The historian might reasonably expect the degree of economic inequality to increase as the agricultural economy of Texas matured and became more productive and complex during the 1850's. On the other hand, the Owsley school argued that the position of the South's plain folk relative to that of the planters improved during the 1850's. In this case, we should find greater economic equality in 1860 than in 1850.

What was the degree of equality or inequality in the distribution of wealth and agricultural property and production in the several geographic regions of Texas in 1850 and 1860? What was the direction and degree of change in the concentration of wealth and agricultural property and production in these regions during that time period? Texas, even that part of the state settled during the antebellum period, covered so vast an area that it contained a number of geographically distinct regions. Generalizations about "antebellum Texas" are likely to have nearly as many exceptions to the rule as there are to general statements about the "antebellum South." To deal with this situation without reducing it to the extreme, we divided the state into four regions and investigated each on the basis of the same questions asked of the whole. (The divisions and the geographical basis for each are explained in chapter 2.) The answers are used to compare each region with the others and with the state as a whole. A comparison of trends in the concentration of wealth and property in older and in more recently settled regions of Texas should be especially suggestive concerning the development of economic classes in a frontier state.

What degree of equality or inequality was there in the distribution of wealth in the urban areas of Texas in 1850 and 1860, and how did concentration of wealth in the towns compare with that in the state as a whole? What was the direction and degree of change in the concentration of wealth in urban areas during the 1850's? Perhaps when measured by the standards of the northeastern United States, Texas had no "urban" areas in 1850 or 1860. Galveston, with a population of 4,117, was the state's largest town in 1850, and San Antonio, with 8,235 residents, was the largest in 1860. Among the other towns of Texas, only Houston and Austin (by 1860) had comparable populations. But however small, these towns were the urban areas of Texas, and it is informative to see how wealth distributions there compared with those for the generally rural state. Existing historical studies lead us to expect a higher degree of inequality in towns and cities. Lee Soltow's book on wealthholding in

Wisconsin demonstrated a significantly higher level of concentration in Milwaukee County than in the state as a whole. Edward Pessen's investigation of the major northeastern cities of New York, Brooklyn, Boston, and Philadelphia before the Civil War, while it did not compare urban and rural wealth distributions, found very high levels of concentration in the cities. If economic inequality thrives in urban areas, it should appear even in the towns of antebellum Texas.[9]

Did the economically elite hold a preponderance of the major political offices and thus dominate Texas politics in 1850 and 1860? Was there any change in the distribution of political officeholding among economic classes during the 1850's? These questions will be answered primarily by comparing the economic status of public officeholders with that of the free population in general. Obviously, there can be no conclusive answer as to whether politics was essentially democratic or aristocratic, but a demonstration of the economic status of the typical officeholder at least suggests which classes of people were in positions that afforded opportunities for the effective use of political power.

How did the distributions of wealth and power in Texas during the 1850's compare with similar measurements for other areas of the antebellum United States? How does the distribution of wealth in Texas during the 1850's compare with distributions of wealth in the twentieth-century United States? A full perspective on the question of economic equality or inequality in antebellum Texas demands comparison not only with the situation existing in other slave states but with that in free areas during the antebellum period and with that in the United States one hundred years after the destruction of slavery. The works of Soltow and Pessen, for example, demonstrate a high level of concentration of wealth and power in Wisconsin and in major cities of the northeast during the

[9]Lee Soltow, *Patterns of Wealthholding in Wisconsin since 1850*, pp. 4-11; Edward Pessen, *Riches, Class, and Power before the Civil War*. Population figures for Texas towns in 1850 and 1860 are in J. D. B. DeBow, *Statistical View of the United States . . . Being a Compendium of the Seventh Census . . .*, pp. 340, 355, 360, 381; and U.S. Bureau of the Census, *Eighth Census of the United States, 1860, Population*, pp. 486-487.

late antebellum years. Perhaps where free populations are concerned, antebellum Texas and the South in general may not have constituted as much of an aristocratic enclave in a democratic republic as is generally believed. Furthermore, although the data necessary for a precise comparison of concentration of wealth in the 1850's with that in the mid-twentieth century are difficult to obtain, such a comparison should prove especially interesting. Perhaps the simpler, preindustrial, agrarian society of the antebellum South was more equalitarian than the more complicated, industrialized, and urbanized United States of the twentieth century. On the other hand, it may be that the South, with its slaveholding elite, was marked by more inequality than twentieth-century America with its massive social welfare programs.

In summary, then, this study of wealth and power in antebellum Texas is intended to investigate all important facets of the planter-dominance versus yeoman-democracy debate concerning the Old South. It must be emphasized again that we are seeking a general interpretation of the economic and political structure of Texas in the 1850's by posing a number of reasonably limited and precise questions. The methods employed in answering these questions will be explained step by step throughout the book. First, however, the methodology of defining the area of study and of collecting data must be described.

Chapter 2.

Texas in the 1850's: A Methodology of Investigation

LURED to Texas by rich, cheap lands and the opportunity to begin a new life, thousands of immigrants from older areas of the United States poured into the Lone Star state in the 1840's and 1850's. The first region most migrants encountered upon arriving in Texas was the east Texas piney woods, stretching from the Red River on the north to the Gulf coastal plain on the south. This area, with climate, vegetation, and terrain similar to that in north Louisiana, Arkansas, and Mississippi, attracted tens of thousands of settlers, mainly from other Southern states, and they continued to grow the same types of crops to which they were accustomed, mainly cotton and corn with some vegetables.

Other new arrivals traveled southward through the eastern forests or arrived by sea to settle in the warm, humid coastal counties of southeastern Texas. With easy access to coastal ports, abundant sun and rainfall, and rich virgin soil, these counties developed into some of the wealthiest in Texas, with huge sugar and cotton plantations providing a slaveholding, landed aristocracy. In addition to boasting the largest plantations and farms in the state, this region also contained two of the few large towns in Texas, Galveston and Houston, where high concentrations of foreign- and Northern-born Texans mingled with old stock Southern Anglo-Saxons. Whereas east Texas was a relatively homogeneous region of small and middling farms and plantations peopled mainly by Southern-born Protestants, coastal Texas was more varied, with huge plantations in some areas, small farms in others, and, settled in the midst of all the fields and slaves, two busy towns rumbling with the sounds of commerce and Yankee, German, Irish, and Southern accents.

Some newcomers, including many Germans, lured westward by stories of rich soil and a less humid climate than that on the Gulf coast, settled on the rolling hills and prairies of south-central Texas. Blessed with adequate rainfall, a long growing season, and access to world markets via both land and water routes, they grew tons of cotton and corn and slaughtered thousands of beeves and swine for their own tables every year. Rubbing shoulders with the aggressive Americans and Germans in this region were many Texans of Mexican birth and Spanish tongue, especially in the large town of San Antonio.

One of the most sparsely populated but fastest growing areas of Texas in the 1850's lay directly north of San Antonio and Austin and west of the eastern forests, the north-central plains stretching out in all directions from the village of Dallas. Drier and slightly cooler than eastern or coastal Texas, the northern plains provided good soil and adequate moisture for cotton cultivation, but sparse population and remoteness from the cotton ports of Galveston and New Orleans kept the region on the edges of the state's cotton empire.

Extending for hundreds of miles beyond all these areas, roughly from the 98th meridian westward, were the dry, wild plains and mountains of western and panhandle Texas. The line of settlement pushing across antebellum Texas did not reach into this western region before the Civil War, and it was generally left to the Indians, buffalo, and some Mexican-born Texans along the Rio Grande.[1]

The great majority of antebellum Texans lived in a vast crescent of counties stretching from the northeastern corner of the state southward to the coastal plain and then looping westward to south-central Texas. Aside from the empty reaches of far west Texas, all regions of the state except

[1]For general descriptions of Texas in the 1850's, see Rupert N. Richardson, Ernest Wallace, and Adrian Anderson, *Texas: The Lone Star State,* and Seymour V. Connor, *Texas, A History.* For information on migration into Texas, see William R. Hogan, *The Texas Republic: A Social and Economic History,* and Barnes F. Lathrop, *Migration into East Texas, 1835-1860: A Study from the United States Census.*

the coastal counties were populated mainly by Southerners in 1850, and natives of the upper South (North Carolina, Virginia, Tennessee, Kentucky, Maryland, Delaware, Missouri, District of Columbia) generally predominated over those of the lower South (Alabama, Arkansas, Florida, Georgia, Louisiana, Mississippi, South Carolina, Texas). The large concentrations of foreign- and Northern-born Texans in Houston and Galveston gave the population of the coastal zone a different look. Indeed, Southerners were a minority there although they predominated in rural areas of the coastal plain. The Lone Star state's population grew rapidly during the 1850's (from 212,592 in 1850 to 604,215 in 1860) and shifted gradually to include a greater proportion of people from the lower South, especially in east Texas, but even by 1860 natives of the upper South constituted the largest single group of Texans (about 40 percent of the free population).[2]

With roughly half a million people scattered over a quarter-million square miles of widely varying terrain and climates, antebellum Texas presents a formidable challenge to the historian. Since we intended to study "antebellum Texas," that portion of the state settled before the Civil War and having an economy and society similar to that in the rest of the Old South, we omitted from consideration the nearly vacant, semiarid plains and mountains of west Texas, roughly from the 98th meridian westward. To include these virtually empty reaches in our calculations would have distorted statistical measurements and concealed more than it revealed about the Lone Star state in the 1850's. We also excluded the small zone between the Rio Grande and Nueces River in far south Texas because it was sparsely settled in the 1850's, due partly to its inhospitably hot, dry climate and partly to confusing, conflicting land claims.[3] In addition, the residents in that area were primarily Mexican-born and

[2]J. D. B. DeBow, ed., *Statistical View of the United States . . ., Being a Compendium of the Seventh Census*, p. 40; U.S. Bureau of the Census, *Eighth Census of the United States, Population*, p. 486, contain statistics on Texas' total population. The other statements about the state's population characteristics are derived from our samples of the state's population drawn from the manuscript census returns. These samples are explained below.

[3]Connor, *Texas, A History*, p. 171.

Spanish-speaking and thus were more an extension of Mexican society than of Texas or Southern society. The two regions omitted from this study contained less than 7 percent of the state's free population and less than 1 percent of the slaves in both 1850 and 1860.[4] Thus, when we speak of Texas in these pages, we refer to the eastern two-fifths of the state, as delineated in figure 1, the Texas that was settled before 1860 and that

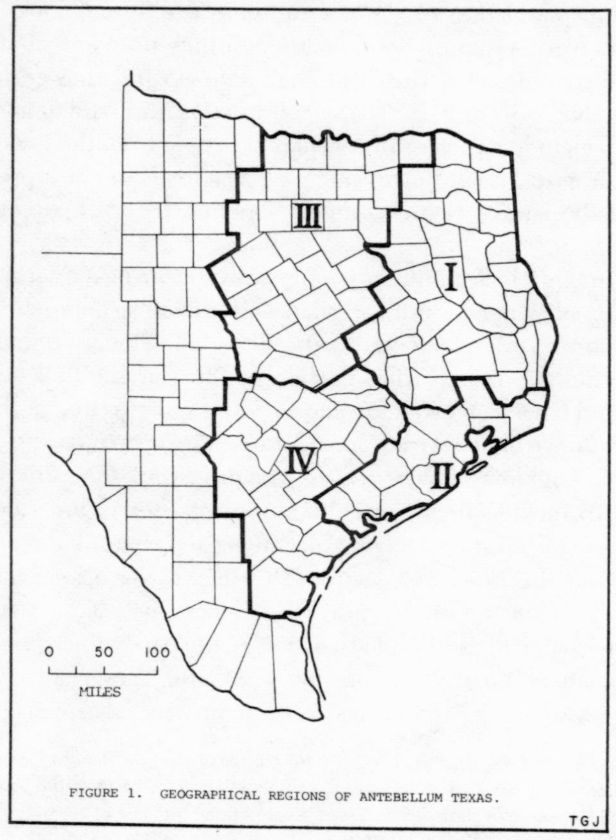

FIGURE 1. GEOGRAPHICAL REGIONS OF ANTEBELLUM TEXAS.

[4]DeBow, ed., *Statistical View of the United States*, pp. 308, 314; *Eighth Census of the United States, Population*, pp. 484-486.

actively participated in the sectional crisis of the 1850's and in the Civil War.

Even when we restrict the investigation to the most meaningful part of the state, however, we are still left with an area about the size of Alabama and Mississippi combined. For purposes of close analysis, then, we divided the state into four regions according to topography, climate, soil types, and vegetation (see figure 1). Region I, eastern Texas, consisting of thirty-six hilly upland counties covered with mixed forests, accounted for 48 percent of antebellum Texas' free population in 1850 and 38 percent in 1860. Region II, slightly warmer coastal Texas, consisting of thirteen coastal plains counties with much rich, alluvial soil, contained 14 percent of the state's free people in 1850 and 9 percent in 1860. Region III, drier and slightly cooler than regions I and II, consisted of thirty-two northern and central prairie counties and held 16 percent of the non-slave population in 1850 and 29 percent in 1860. Finally, region IV, twenty-four central and southern prairie and plains counties with less rainfall than regions I and II, contained 22 percent of the free people in 1850 and 24 percent in 1860.[5]

Sampling Procedure

Once we had defined our "universe" (i.e., the total population under study) and subdivided it into four geographical regions, we took a random

[5]Information on the geographical characteristics of each region is in "The General Soil Map of Texas, 1973," Texas Agricultural Experiment Station, Texas A&M University, College Station, Texas, 1973; and *Texas Almanac and State Industrial Guide, 1970-1971*, pp. 103, 105, 116-119, 127-132. The number of counties in each region is the number as of 1860. Some further justification for our geographical divisions is necessary. Lathrop, in his study of migration into east Texas, used the Trinity River, a political boundary dividing the eastern and western congressional districts, to define east Texas. But, in general, geographical factors such as rainfall and soil types have more impact on economic and social life than do political boundaries; we therefore judged them more appropriate for our purposes. Other historians have recognized the importance of geographical criteria. See, for example, Gavin Wright, " 'Economic Democracy' and the Concentration of Agricultural Wealth in the Cotton South, 1850-1860," *Agricultural History* 44 (January 1970), 63-93; and Donald W. Meinig, *Imperial Texas: An Interpretive Essay in Cultural Geography*, who used geographical divisions remarkably similar to those employed in our study.

sample of 5,000 heads of families for 1850 and 5,000 for 1860 from the manuscript United States census records for those years.[6] A sample of 5,000 is large enough to reduce sampling error to near zero. In addition, because we wanted to study smaller groups within the total universe, such as slaveholding farmers, the various regions, and the urban population, we needed a sample of about 5,000 to ensure that these smaller subgroups would be large enough to study with little fear of sampling error.[7]

To be certain that our sample was truly random and thus an unbiased picture of antebellum Texas, we secured two lists (one for 1850 and one for 1860) of 5,000 numbers chosen at random by an IBM computer. Each list was divided into four groups of numbers (one group for each of our regions) weighted to correspond to the proportion of free population in each region in 1850 and in 1860. For example, region II contained 13.6 percent of the state's free population in 1850; we therefore secured 680 random numbers (13.6 percent of 5,000) for region II's share of the total 1850 sample.[8] With the counties of each region arranged in random order, we proceeded through the manuscript census records for those counties using the lists of random numbers to indicate which families should be included in our sample. For example, the first number in our computer-generated list for region I in 1850 was five. The first county in our random ordering of region I's counties was Upshur. Therefore, we

[6]Although the samples were based on heads of families, throughout this study we use the terms "heads of families" and "heads of households" interchangeably. Census enumerators numbered households and families separately and in a few cases there was more than one family in a single household. In such cases, our sample took the appropriately numbered family rather than the household. Such cases were so few, however, that we felt justified in using the terms interchangeably.

[7]Charles M. Dollar and Richard J. Jensen, *Historian's Guide to Statistics: Quantitative Analysis and Historical Research*, pp. 13-14.

[8]There were a total of 3,553 families in region II from which we were to take our sample of 680. We therefore asked the computer to generate 680 random numbers from 1 to 3,553. These numbers then determined which of the 3,553 families would be included in our sample.

proceeded through the free population census for Upshur County until we reached the fifth family whereupon we gathered basic information on the head of that family. This process continued through every county in all four regions until each of the 5,000 random numbers was matched with a household. The entire process was then repeated with a new random ordering of the counties and a new list of random numbers for 1860. Thus, our sample was random and unbiased in that every family in antebellum Texas had an equal chance of being selected. It was large enough virtually to eliminate sampling error, large enough to provide sizable subsamples for analysis, and stratified according to the proportion of free population in each region in each census year.[9]

Once we knew which heads of household to include in our sample, we collected census data for each from three census schedules. Schedule I contains information on the entire free population, including name, age, sex, race, occupation, the amount of real and personal property owned, place of birth, and an indication of whether adults were literate or not. Having recorded this for our sample heads of households, we turned to Schedule II, which contains the names of every slaveowner and the number of slaves he held. If our sample head of household owned slaves, we recorded the number of his bondsmen. Finally, we searched through Schedule IV, which contains extensive data on each farm in the state, including the number of improved and unimproved acres on the farm, the cash value of the farm, the value of farm implements and livestock, and the size of the various crops. If our sample head of household appeared in this agricultural schedule, we recorded the data for his farm. Thus, all members of our sample appeared in Schedule I; those who were slaveowners appeared again in Schedule II; and those who operated farms appeared again in Schedule IV.[10]

[9]We wish to thank Professor Charles M. Dollar of the National Archives for his suggestion that we use a computer-generated, stratified, random sample for this study.

[10]Full descriptions of these schedules are in Carroll D. Wright, *The History and Growth of the United States Census*, pp. 147-154, 234-237. The census of 1850 did not record the value of personal property, but it was included in 1860. We used the manuscript returns of the Seventh Census of the United States, 1850, Schedule I (Free Inhabitants),

This approach, searching through three different census schedules for each of 10,000 names, presents some problems. One of the most frustrating resulted from the unfortunate decision by a few census enumerators to take short cuts in their work that made their manuscript returns virtually useless for our purposes. We had to drop from consideration three counties in 1850 and two in 1860 because the census takers, rather than following directions, filled out the agricultural schedule in a manner apparently intelligible only to themselves. Although irritating, these omissions probably had little effect on our statistical measurements for three reasons: they included only 137 cases (i.e., heads of households) out of 5,000 in 1850 and 79 out of 5,000 in 1860 (2.7 percent and 1.6 percent of the two samples); the omitted cases did not fall in any one wealth category but were spread out over several; and the counties omitted were not concentrated in any one region.

A less serious problem involved individuals who listed their occupations as "farmer" in Schedule I but could not be found in Schedule IV, the agricultural schedule. In some cases, however, these individuals held little or no real property, indicating that they probably worked on someone else's farm rather than operated their own. In other cases, when these individuals did own real property, they may have lived in town while an overseer or son operated the farm. In all cases, the person who operated the farm, whether overseer, relative, or tenant, appeared in the agricultural schedule.[11] Another problem occasionally arose when the figures for a sample head of household were clearly internally inconsistent. For example, an individual who claimed to own no personal property may have appeared in the slave schedule with several bondsmen, a valuable form of personal property. In some cases, census enumerators

Schedule II (Slave Inhabitants), and Schedule IV (Productions of Agriculture) and of the Eighth Census of the United States, 1860, Schedules I, II, and IV on microfilm. Hereinafter these manuscript returns will be cited as Seventh Census, 1850, and Eighth Census, 1860, with appropriate schedules.

[11]Wright, *History and Growth of the United States Census*, p. 45.

refused to record the cash value of a farm if the farm operator was not the owner.

Whenever there was no obvious mistake by the census taker or respondent in these questionable cases, we recorded them as they appeared. When there *was* clearly an error, however, we substituted another head of household for the questionable one. In such instances, we used two criteria in selecting substitutes: close proximity in the free population schedule and comparable age, place of birth, and property figures. In summary, data collection for 10,000 cases obviously involves the possibility of some degree of error. But problem cases were relatively few, and they probably affect our statistical measurements very little if at all, especially in such a large sample.

One problem for which we made a specific adjustment involved people with more than one occupation. Many Texans, especially merchants, lawyers, and carpenters, listed their occupations as "merchant," "lawyer," or "carpenter" in Schedule I, and yet they appeared with farms in the agricultural schedule, indicating that they were pursuing more than one occupation. If we had included only the self-professed farmers in our analysis of the agricultural population, we would have been omitting from consideration many important farmers.

Therefore, in order to have a systematic breakdown of the entire sample and to be certain that we had analyzed the entire agricultural population, we recorded each person's occupation as he listed it himself, but then we also placed every person in the sample in one of our own six broad occupational categories. The six categories were the following: slaveholding farmers who had farms listed in the agricultural schedule; slaveholding farmers who were not listed as having a farm; non-slaveholding farmers who had listed farms; non-slaveholding farmers who were not listed as having a farm; slaveholding non-farmers; and non-slaveholding non-farmers. All farmers of whatever type are included in the first four groups, and all non-farmers in the fifth and sixth groups. With this dual system we have occupations as given by the respondents and also a systematic breakdown of the entire sample according to whether they were farmers or non-farmers and whether they were slaveholders or non-slaveholders.

Reliability of Data and the Samples

Once we had gathered census data on all family heads in our samples for 1850 and 1860 and had the data keypunched onto IBM cards, we subjected all the cards (two cards per household or "case") to three computer programs designed to detect clerical and keypunch errors. The correction of these mistakes left our data as "clean" as possible of mechanical errors. There still remained two questions concerning the overall quality of our data: how reliable and valid is statistical information drawn from the United States censuses of 1850 and 1860, and were our samples representative of the populations of Texas reported in these censuses?

The first question, which existed of course from the outset of our study, is most difficult to answer where it concerned direct measures of wealthholding, such as the value of each individual's real estate recorded in Schedule I. It must be noted first that the census marshals who collected this information were given basically sensible and unambiguous instructions. In 1850, they were directed to insert under heading 8 of Schedule I

> the value of real estate owned by each individual enumerated. You are to obtain the value of real estate by inquiry of each individual who is supposed to own real estate, be the same located where it may, and insert the amount in dollars. No abatement of the value is to be made on account of any lien or incumbrance thereon in the nature of debt.

The 1860 instructions for recording the value of real estate were essentially the same. For personal estate the directions read as follows:

> Under heading 9, insert (in dollars) the value of personal property or estate. Here you are to include the value of all the property, possessions, or wealth of each individual which is not embraced in the column previous, consist of what it may; the value of bonds, mortgages, notes, slaves, live stock, plate, jewels, or furniture; in fine, the value of whatever constitutes the personal wealth of individuals. Exact accuracy may not be arrived at, but all persons should be encouraged to give a near and prompt estimate for your informa-

tion. Should any respondent manifest hesitancy or unwillingness to make a free reply on these or any other subject, you will direct attention to Nos. 6 and 13 of your general instructions and the 15th section of the law.[12]

Difficulties arise of course under the most precise instructions. Joint ownership of property, for example, could lead to confusion, as could situations where an individual controlling property in Texas was actually working as an agent for owners in another state. It seems likely too that some individuals, acting out of suspicion of government or fear of the tax collector, undervalued their property while others bolstered their egos with exaggerated figures. There were, however, few cases of complex property holding arrangements in an economy as simple as that of antebellum Texas. Also, census information was entirely confidential, and there were no pervasive reasons for deliberate misrepresentation of wealthholding.[13]

Thus the circumstances under which the censuses of 1850 and 1860 were conducted allow us to expect reasonable accuracy in the data on real and personal estate. Historians and economists, including Robert Gallman, the pioneer investigator of wealth distribution data from the census returns, have generally agreed that both enumerators and respondents met their obligations well.[14] Certainly information from the censuses is the best historical source available on antebellum wealthholding.

There are fewer questions concerning the validity and reliability of data drawn from Schedule II (Slave Inhabitants) and Schedule IV (Products of Agriculture) of the census returns. Occasionally, due to such practices as hiring out, it is difficult to match slaves with their true owner or

[12]Instructions for 1850 are in Wright, *History and Growth of the United States Census*, p. 152; those for 1860 are reprinted in Lee Soltow, *Patterns of Wealthholding in Wisconsin since 1850*, pp. 141-145.

[13]The personal information in the 1850 and 1860 manuscript censuses was not released to the public until the 1940's. See Soltow, *Patterns of Wealthholding in Wisconsin*, p. 19.

[14]Robert E. Gallman, "Trends in the Size Distribution of Wealth in the Nineteenth Century: Some Speculations," in Lee Soltow, ed., *Six Papers on the Size Distribution of Wealth and Income*, pp. 16-17.

place of residence, but in general the slave population was reported with acceptable accuracy. A limited comparison of individual slaveholdings reported in Schedule II for Harrison County, the largest slaveholding county in the state, with slaveholdings listed in the state tax returns of the same individuals during the census years revealed close agreement on the number of bondsmen given in two distinct records.[15] Thus it seems reasonable, and most historians over the years have agreed, that these census data are a valid and reliable source of information for historical investigation of the slave population.

In the case of Schedule IV, there are, as noted above, some difficulties involved in properly identifying the actual owners of farms with their agricultural property, and some farms reported data that were internally inconsistent. But once these problem cases are disposed of there is little question concerning the general acceptability of the figures reported for agricultural property and products. Economic historians, for example, may still debate the actual weight of a bale of cotton reported in the census, but they accept and work with the information provided on total production. There are no other such sources, and there is no evidence that the statistics presented in Schedule IV are especially biased in any direction. Thus, these data seem reliable and valid for the purposes of our investigation into the distribution of agricultural wealth in 1850 and 1860.

The second question concerns the validity of our sample data drawn from the census records. Were the samples for 1850 and 1860 truly representative of the universes from which they were drawn? Or, in other words, were there statistically significant differences between our sample populations and the universe populations? Employing universe data totals drawn from the published census returns, several methods were used to test our samples and answer this question.

The first method employed to test for statistically significant differences between our samples on the one hand and the universes on the

[15]Seventh Census, 1850, Schedule II; Eighth Census, 1860, Schedule II; Records of the Comptroller of Public Accounts, Ad Valorem Tax Division; County Real and Personal Tax Rolls, 1836-1874, Archives Division, Texas State Library, Austin.

other hand was the familiar t-test.[16] Although hampered in a few cases by the lack of adequate universe data, we were able to test the reliability of our 1850 sample for size of slaveholding, improved acreage, unimproved acreage, corn, cotton, other grain, food crops, cheese and butter, and value of livestock slaughtered.[17] For every one of these items except cotton, the results of the t-test indicated that there was no statistically significant difference between our 1850 sample and the universe. In other words, the sample was representative of the universe. In the case of cotton, our sample mean (3.57 bales per farm) was probably biased downward very slightly. (The universe mean was 4.2 bales, only a fraction of a bale more than our sample mean.)

For the 1860 sample we applied the t-test to real property, personal property, size of slaveholding, improved and unimproved acreage, cash value of farm, value of farm implements, value of livestock, corn, other grain, cotton, food crops, butter and cheese, value of home manufactures, and value of animals slaughtered. With the exceptions of size of slaveholding, value of livestock, and butter and cheese, the results indicated no statistically significant differences between our sample and the universe. In the case of livestock value, our mean was biased upward slightly from that of the universe; in the case of cheese and butter production, slightly downward. Where size of slaveholding is concerned, our sample mean (9.4 slaves per slaveholding household) was higher than the universe mean (8.3 slaves per slaveholder). This is only to be expected, however, because we measured the number of slaves *per household* whereas the universe data were based on the number of slaves *per individual*

[16]For a description of the t-test and its formula, see Janet T. Spence et al., *Elementary Statistics*, chapter 8. Spence describes the t-formula as a form of the z-formula.

[17]We could not test the reliability of sample figures on real property and value of livestock because the published census returns for 1850 did not include county-level data on these items, and we were therefore unable to determine exact universe totals and means. The 1850 published returns presented cash value of farms and value of farm equipment as one combined item, whereas we included them in our sample as separate items. We therefore had no standard deviations for the combined item, and since the standard deviation is a necessary element in calculating the t-statistic, we could not test these two items.

slaveholder. In most cases, slaveholders who were not heads of households owned few slaves, and when they are included in the calculations (as in the universe data) they lower the mean size of slaveholding. The difference between the two means was so slight that we believe that, if the universe and sample means had been calculated in exactly the same way, our sample mean would not be significantly different from the universe mean.

Another method of testing the representativeness of the samples was to compare the samples as proportions of the universes. For example, if our sample included a particular percentage of the farms in the universe, we would expect our sample to include a comparable percentage of the improved acreage in the universe. In 1850 our sample included 18.8 percent of the families in the universe, 18.9 percent of the slaveholders, and 18.9 percent of the slaves. It included 20.8 percent of the universe farms, and all other farm figures (e.g., improved acreage, unimproved acreage) except cotton were within two percentage points of 20.8 percent. As expected from our t-test, our sample contained slightly less cotton (17.8 percent) than it should have.

The 1860 sample included 7.1 percent of all universe families, 6.24 percent of the slaveholders, and 7.05 percent of the slaves in the universe. The figure on slaveholders (6.24 percent) is lower than the 7.1 percent of all families, but this is explained by our sample's counting of households rather than individual slaveholders. The sample also included 7.98 percent of all farms in the universe, and all our farm figures are within 1 percent of the 7.98 percent.

Thus, on the basis of the t-tests and of the comparisons of samples as proportions of the universe, we conclude that our samples are valid representations of "antebellum Texas" as defined for the purposes of this study.

To summarize, then, our method of investigation involved the following steps: (1) determining the area to be studied as antebellum Texas, (2) selecting a random sample of 5,000 cases (heads of households) from the censuses of 1850 and 1860 for antebellum Texas, (3) identifying all cases in Schedule I of the census and where possible in Schedules II and

IV and collecting full data on each case from each schedule, (4) having the data keypunched on IBM cards and "cleaning" it of clerical and keypunch errors, and (5) testing the reliability of the 1850 and 1860 samples.

The Sample Populations

At this point we are ready to turn attention from the procedures of structuring our investigation and collecting data to analysis of the material collected. Our first task was to break the two samples (1850 and 1860) down into our six broad slaveholder-occupation categories. Table 1 demonstrates that nearly 80 percent of the state's population in 1850 and about 75 percent in 1860 were directly involved in farming of one type or another. (Hereinafter all references to the "state population," "statewide population," and so on, unless otherwise indicated, apply to our total sample population.) Add to this the thousands of Texans in occupations supporting agriculture, such as cotton gin operators and manufacturers, harness and plow makers, and agents, and it becomes clear that the interests of farmers and planters were paramount in the Lone Star state. Table 1 also shows that region II (the coastal plain) and region III (the north-central plains) deviated farthest from the statewide pattern in both 1850 and 1860. Region II, which included the large towns of Galveston and Houston, had relatively fewer farmers and proportionally more non-farmers than other areas of the state. Region III, the more sparsely settled and less developed area in north-central Texas, had a lower proportion of slaveholders and a higher proportion of non-slaveholding farmers than the state as a whole. Regions I (east Texas) and IV (the south-central counties) were more comparable to the statewide pattern, although they did differ from it in some details.[18]

In addition to the description of slaveholding and general occupational status, the sample family heads may also be characterized according

[18]The figures discussed here and presented in table 1 are from our samples drawn from Schedules I, II, and IV of the 1850 and 1860 manuscript census returns. Hereinafter, all statistical data in the text, unless otherwise cited, are taken from our samples.

TABLE 1

SAMPLE POPULATIONS FOR 1850 AND 1860

1850

	Whole Sample		Region I		Region II		Region III		Region IV	
	No.	%	No.	%	No.	%	No.	%	No.	%
Slaveholding Farmers with Farms	1,156	23.8	652	28.6	150	22.1	136	16.5	218	20.3
Slaveholding Farmers without Farms	102	2.1	81	3.5	7	1.0	3	0.3	11	1.0
Non-Slaveholding Farmers with Farms	1,893	38.9	912	39.9	124	18.2	517	62.6	340	31.7
Non-Slaveholding Farmers without Farms	617	12.7	356	15.6	59	8.7	99	12.0	103	9.6
Slaveholding Non-Farmers	207	4.2	79	3.5	67	9.9	6	0.7	55	5.1
Non-Slaveholding Non-Farmers	888	18.3	203	8.9	273	40.1	65	7.9	347	32.3
Total	4,863	100.0	2,283	100.0	680	100.0	826	100.0	1,074	100.0

1860

	Whole Sample		Region I		Region II		Region III		Region IV	
	No.	%	No.	%	No.	%	No.	%	No.	%
Slaveholding Farmers with Farms	1,117	22.7	563	29.8	78	17.4	233	16.8	243	20.4
Slaveholding Farmers without Farms	62	1.3	24	1.3	5	1.1	20	1.4	13	1.0
Non-Slaveholding Farmers with Farms	1,841	37.4	740	39.1	54	12.1	614	44.2	433	36.3
Non-Slaveholding Farmers without Farms	640	13.0	220	11.6	12	2.7	274	19.7	134	11.2
Slaveholding Non-Farmers	162	3.3	62	3.3	45	10.1	23	1.6	32	2.7
Non-Slaveholding Non-Farmers	1,099	22.3	281	14.9	253	56.6	226	16.3	339	28.4
Total	4,921	100.0	1,890	100.0	447	100.0	1,390	100.0	1,194	100.0

to age, birthplace, and specific occupation. Heads of households in antebellum Texas were quite young by twentieth-century standards. They averaged only 38.1 years each in 1850 and 39.0 in 1860. By comparison, adult males in the United States in 1970, whether they were heads of households or not, were 44 years of age on the average.[19] Mean ages in the four regions of antebellum Texas did not vary as much as a year from the statewide figure.

Table 2 presents a breakdown of the sample populations according to place of birth. Natives of the South constituted more than three-fourths of all sample family heads in both 1850 and 1860. They were a majority in every region except Gulf coastal Texas (region II), where large numbers of the foreign-born and natives of the free states congregated in the towns of Galveston and Houston. Among Southerners, those born in the upper South were more numerous, but lower Southerners gained noticeably

TABLE 2

PLACES OF BIRTH OF HEADS OF HOUSEHOLDS

(In Percentages)

	1850					1860				
	Texas	Region I	Region II	Region III	Region IV	Texas	Region I	Region II	Region III	Region IV
Lower South*	30.2	38.8	23.7	18.8	24.8	36.0	51.6	26.4	27.3	25.0
Upper South*	45.6	52.3	22.8	64.3	31.4	41.1	41.1	19.7	58.4	29.1
Free States	9.5	5.5	18.1	14.7	8.6	8.1	4.5	14.1	11.7	7.4
Foreign-Born	14.2	2.8	35.4	1.2	35.0	14.5	2.5	39.6	2.0	38.4
Unknown	0.5	0.6	0.0	1.0	0.2	0.3	0.3	0.2	0.6	0.1
Total	100.0	100.0	100.0	100.0	100.0	100.0	100.0	100.0	100.0	100.0

* Alabama, Arkansas, Florida, Georgia, Louisiana, Mississippi, South Carolina, Texas

** Delaware, District of Columbia, Kentucky, Maryland, Missouri, North Carolina, Tennessee, Virginia

[19]Lee Soltow, *Men and Wealth in the United States, 1850-1870*, p. 9.

during the 1850's. Natives of the free states made up less than 10 percent of all sample heads of households in both census years. They were a larger proportion in regions II and III, but in no area were they as much as one-fifth of the total. The foreign-born remained stable at about one-seventh of the total sample in both 1850 and 1860. They were, however, a significant proportion (more than one-third) in regions II and IV, where

TABLE 3

OCCUPATIONS OF HEADS OF HOUSEHOLDS

(In Percentages)

	1850					1860				
	Texas	Region I	Region II	Region III	Region IV	Texas	Region I	Region II	Region III	Region IV
Farming	71.0	80.1	45.6	82.9	58.5	69.0	77.0	30.9	76.0	62.4
Commerce	3.8	2.6	9.4	1.5	4.7	4.3	3.0	12.8	3.1	4.8
Professions	5.4	5.0	9.1	4.0	4.8	5.0	4.7	6.3	4.8	5.2
Public Office	0.7	0.7	1.5	0.1	0.7	0.8	0.8	1.3	0.8	0.7
Manufacturing	1.1	1.4	0.9	1.2	0.6	1.1	1.1	1.1	1.4	0.9
Skilled Trades	10.9	6.8	22.5	8.5	14.0	9.2	5.8	18.8	8.1	11.8
Unskilled Services	5.8	2.1	8.7	1.0	15.5	9.2	6.2	23.7	5.5	12.6
Overseer	0.3	0.4	0.4	-	0.2	0.7	1.0	0.9	0.1	1.0
Miscellaneous	1.0	0.9	1.9	0.8	1.0	0.7	0.4	4.2	0.1	0.6
Total	100.0	100.0	100.0	100.0	100.0	100.0	100.0	100.0	100.0	100.0

the largest Texas towns of Galveston, Houston, San Antonio, and Austin were located.

The occupational statuses of the sample family heads are presented in table 3. As should be expected, farmers were a clear majority (more than two-thirds) of the sample in both years. Only region II differed from this rule. The next most numerous occupational groups were the skilled tradesmen (including such occupations as blacksmith, ginwright, and tailor) and unskilled workers (including such jobs as day laborer, clerk, and wagoner), who together constituted nearly one-fifth of all household heads. Regions II and IV, with their towns, had noticeably larger proportions of skilled and unskilled workers. The remaining 10 to 15 percent of the sample were scattered among the other occupations.

Tables 1, 2, and 3 simply describe the basic characteristics of our sample populations. An analysis of the distribution of wealth among these antebellum Texans (statewide and in each region) is the subject of our next chapter.

Chapter 3.

Wealthholding in Texas, 1850-1860

THE United States censuses of 1850 and 1860 provide basic data on the distribution of wealth among the entire free population of antebellum Texas. In 1850 census takers listed in Schedule I the dollar value of all the real estate owned by each person enumerated. Ten years later this schedule was broadened to include the value of every individual's personal estate, an item that included all property not evaluated as real estate, such as slaves, bonds, mortgages, and jewelry. Slaves were enumerated according to owner in Schedule II of both censuses. This schedule does not provide dollar valuations of the bondsmen listed, but it does permit the consideration of slaves — a unique but especially important kind of wealth — apart from other forms of property.

Although census data on wealth are less comprehensive for 1850, when only real estate was evaluated, than for 1860, when values were recorded for both real estate and personal property, the information for 1850 is certainly full enough to provide strong indications of the degree of equality or inequality in overall wealthholding in that census year. It is likely that the real estate values constituted nearly one-half of all wealth, and slaves, which were enumerated in Schedule II, were by far the largest and most valuable part of the other property that fell into the unrecorded category of personal estate. Thus, the distributions of real estate and slave property, although they cannot be defined as a complete measure of wealth in Texas, are very good indicators of the concentration of wealth in general in 1850. And they are directly comparable with measures of concentration in real estate and slave holdings drawn from the 1860 census. Accordingly, distributions of real estate and slave property from the censuses of 1850 and 1860 will be presented, analyzed, and compared. Then for 1860, evaluations of personal property will also be presented as an indicator of the degree of concentration in wealthholding. Finally, the evaluations of real and personal estate (which included the value of slaves) will be combined to provide a comprehensive measure of wealth and its distribution in 1860.

Real Property, 1850-1860

Tables 4 and 5 present a full breakdown of all the data necessary to demonstrate the distribution of real property in 1850. Every individual in the sample population is placed in one of six classes according to his slaveholding and occupational status. (These classes, such as slaveholding farmer, non-slaveholding non-farmer, etc., are described in detail in chapter 2.) The individuals in each class are then arranged in nine intervals determined by the value of their real estate holdings ($1,000 to $4,999, for example), and the result is table 4, a six-by-nine cross tabulation of real estate holdings according to slaveholder-occupational class. Next the total value of the real property held by all the individuals in each cell of the cross tabulation is determined (table 5). And finally, the total number of real property owners in each interval and the total value of their holdings are converted to percentages. We can now see, for example, that 1,678 individuals constituting 34.5 percent of the sample population owned no real property while the richest 13, who constituted 0.3 percent of the sample, held $50,000 or more each and controlled 13.0 percent of all the real property. As another example, only 230 of the 1,678 individuals who had no real estate were slaveholders (128 slaveholding farmers with farms, 55 slaveholding farmers without farms, and 47 non-farmer slaveholders). At the same time, 12 of the richest 13 persons owned property in slaves.

Tables 6 and 7 demonstrate a repetition of this process for the distribution of real estate in 1860. They show, for example, that while the percentage of the population owning no real estate had decreased slightly since 1850 to 33.1 percent (1,629 individuals), the richest group had

TABLE 4

DISTRIBUTION OF REAL PROPERTY: NUMBER OF REAL PROPERTY HOLDERS ACCORDING TO VALUE OF PROPERTY, 1850

Value of Real Property	0	$1–249	$250–499	$500–999	$1,000–4,999	$5,000–9,999	$10,000 19,999	$20,000–49,999	$50,000+	Totals
Slaveholding Farmer with Farm	128	42	80	167	510	122	75	23	9	1,156
Slaveholding Farmer without Farm	55	6	9	12	19	0	0	1	0	102
Non-Slaveholding Farmer with Farm	469	285	344	376	368	38	11	2	0	1,893
Non-Slaveholding Farmer without Farm	485	68	36	22	6	0	0	0	0	617
Slaveholding Non-Farmer	47	4	9	21	75	28	13	7	3	207
Non-Slaveholding Non-Farmer	494	117	74	81	103	12	6	0	1	888
Totals	1,678	522	552	679	1,081	200	105	33	13	4,863
Percentage of Total	34.5	10.7	11.4	14.0	22.2	4.1	2.2	0.7	0.3	100

TABLE 5

DISTRIBUTION OF REAL PROPERTY: TOTAL VALUE OF REAL PROPERTY HELD, 1850

Value of Real Property	0	$1-249	$250-499	$500-999	$1,000-4,999	$5,000-9,999	$10,000-19,999	$20,000 49,999	$50,000+	Totals
Slaveholding Farmer with Farm	0	7,485	27,930	115,075	1,050,084	761,190	949,919	588,678	712,304	4,212,665
Slaveholding Farmer with-out Farm	0	1,012	2,925	7,820	33,662	0	0	20,000	0	65,419
Non-Slave-holding Farmer with Farm	0	42,891	115,314	239,619	650,601	238,856	125,519	60,000	0	1,472,800
Non-Slave-holding Farmer without Farm	0	9,078	12,141	13,566	9,367	0	0	0	0	44,142
Slaveholding Non-Farmer	0	750	3,430	12,765	154,579	179,770	142,000	195,700	160,000	848,994
Non-Slave-holding Non-Farmer	0	15,528	23,910	49,259	175,557	70,610	78,800	0	50,000	463,664
Totals	0	76,744	185,650	438,094	2,073,850	1,250,426	1,296,238	864,378	922,304	7,107,684
Percentage of Total	0.0	1.1	2.6	6.2	29.2	17.6	18.2	12.2	13.0	100

TABLE 6

DISTRIBUTION OF REAL PROPERTY: NUMBER OF REAL PROPERTY HOLDERS ACCORDING TO VALUE OF PROPERTY, 1860

Value of Real Property	0	$1-249	$250-499	$500-999	$1,000-4,999	$5,000-9,999	$10,000 19,999	$20,000 49,999	$50,000+	Totals
Slaveholding Farmer with Farm	52	8	28	68	547	184	136	72	22	1,117
Slaveholding Farmer without Farm	55	0	3	2	1	0	1	0	0	62
Non-Slaveholding Farmer with Farm	252	127	293	438	668	41	20	2	0	1,841
Non-Slaveholding Farmer without Farm	591	23	6	5	12	0	2	1	0	640
Slaveholding Non-Farmer	21	1	7	12	59	25	14	14	9	162
Non-Slaveholding Non-Farmer	658	48	80	108	172	14	10	4	5	1,099
Totals	1,629	207	417	633	1,459	264	183	93	36	4,921
Percentage of Total	33.1	4.2	8.5	12.9	29.7	5.4	3.7	1.9	0.7	100

TABLE 7

DISTRIBUTION OF REAL PROPERTY: TOTAL VALUE OF REAL PROPERTY HELD, 1860

Value of Real Property	0	$1–249	$250–499	$500–999	$1,000–4,999	$5,000–9,999	$10,000–19,999	$20,000–49,999	$50,000+	Totals
Slaveholding Farmer with Farm	0	1,285	10,740	48,238	1,293,795	1,170,602	1,737,388	2,113,632	1,768,878	8,144,558
Slaveholding Farmer without Farm	0	0	1,250	1,373	1,500	0	15,000	0	0	19,123
Non-Slaveholding Farmer with Farm	0	20,906	103,551	290,850	1,232,778	252,228	263,939	46,533	0	2,210,785
Non-Slaveholding Farmer without Farm	0	2,750	2,100	3,481	24,130	0	21,105	30,000	0	83,566
Slaveholding Non-Farmer	0	200	2,500	7,940	136,240	159,620	170,450	390,680	851,000	1,718,630
Non-Slaveholding Non-Farmer	0	6,717	27,164	69,434	328,163	88,900	131,465	105,000	349,024	1,105,867
Totals	0	31,858	147,305	421,316	3,016,606	1,671,350	2,339,347	2,685,845	2,968,902	13,282,529
Percentage of Total	0.0	0.2	1.1	3.2	22.7	12.6	17.6	20.2	22.4	100

increased sharply to 0.7 percent (36 persons) of the total and now held 22.4 percent of all real estate.

Thus tables 4 through 7 present all the data required for a class by class, interval by interval analysis and comparison of the distributions of real estate in 1850 and 1860. These tables are an essential step in the investigation, but they are unnecessarily detailed and cumbersome for presentation of the more generally significant points concerning concentration in real property holdings. Table 8, a simplified combination of the material used in tables 4 through 7, is more easily understood and more effective in demonstrating the distribution of real estate in 1850 and 1860 because it presents the important information in percentage form for the whole sample population. For example, table 8 shows that 34.5 percent of the whole sample owned no real estate in 1850. Another 10.7 percent of the sample owned real estate valued at $1 to $249, and their share of real property amounted to 1.1 percent of the total.

TABLE 8

DISTRIBUTION OF REAL PROPERTY IN ANTEBELLUM TEXAS, 1850 AND 1860

$ Value of Real Property	0	1-249	250-499	500-999	1,000-4,999	5,000-9,999	10,000-19,999	20,000-49,999	50,000+	Totals
1850										
% of Population	34.5	10.7	11.3	14.0	22.2	4.1	2.2	0.7	0.3	100.0
% of Real Property	0.0	1.1	2.6	6.1	29.2	17.6	18.2	12.2	13.0	100.0
1860										
% of Population	33.1	4.2	8.5	12.9	29.6	5.4	3.7	1.9	0.7	100.0
% of Real Property	0.0	0.2	1.1	3.2	22.7	12.6	17.6	20.2	22.4	100.0

To conserve space and strive for clarity on the important points, most statistical information in this study will be presented and analyzed in percentage form as in table 8. Obviously there is little use in presenting the absolute number of individuals or the absolute value of property for a particular interval, especially when the numbers are derived from a sample. Valid comparisons are not readily apparent, for example, from a demonstration that 13 individuals in the $50,000 or more interval owned $922,304 worth of real estate in 1850 and that by 1860 this group had increased to 36 persons who held $2,968,902 in real property. Instead, analysis and comparisons must be made primarily in terms of the percentages of the population in the various intervals and their proportional shares of the property in question. Therefore, this investigation of the degree of equality or inequality of wealthholding in antebellum Texas is made largely in terms of the relative status of economic groups, not in terms of absolute numbers of people or absolute values of the property held by them.

Table 8 reveals a noticeably unequal distribution of real estate in both 1850 and 1860. The least wealthy group, those owning real property worth less than $250, constituted 45.2 percent of the sample population in 1850 and held only 1.1 percent of all real property. Ten years later this class had declined to 37.3 percent, but their share of real estate had dropped even more sharply to 0.2 percent of the total. In the same period, the group with middle-sized holdings ranging from $250 to $9,999 increased from 51.6 percent to 56.4 percent of the sample, but their share of real estate declined sharply from 55.5 percent to 39.6 percent of the total. The richest group, individuals owning $10,000 or more in real property, increased from 3.2 percent to 6.3 percent of the sample and their share of real estate advanced from 43.4 percent to 60.2 percent.[1] It

[1]The statistics in this paragraph for the three wealthholding groups are derived by combining the percentage figures in the cells of table 8. For example, the 3.2 percent for the richest group in 1850 is a combination of the 2.2 percent who owned $10,000 to $19,999, the 0.7 percent who owned $20,000 to $49,999, and the 0.3 percent who owned $50,000 or more of real property.

seems clear that a small wealthy group held a disproportionate share of real property in both 1850 and 1860.

The question now becomes, exactly what degree of concentration in the ownership of real estate was represented by conditions among our sample populations in 1850 and 1860? Tables 4 through 8 indicate a maldistribution in favor of a wealthy group composed of less than 10 percent of the whole. But they do not permit precise comparisons of the changing degree of inequality from 1850 to 1860 or comparisons of concentration in real estate with the situation in slaveholding, ownership of personal property, and so forth. Thus, it becomes necessary to reduce the conditions represented in these tables to a standard measure through use of the Lorenz curve and the Gini index of concentration. This process is illustrated for the distribution of real property in figure 2. Percentages of the population are plotted along the vertical *(Y)* axis while percentages of real estate value are plotted along the horizontal *(X)* axis. Under conditions of perfect equality in the distribution of real estate, each 1 percent of the sample population would own 1 percent of the value of all real estate. The result would be a straight line *(Z)* at forty-five degrees. However, when the actual percentages from table 8 are plotted, the results are curves well above the straight line of perfect equality. The general rule for visually interpreting the Lorenz curve is that the bow of the curve becomes greater as concentration increases.[2] In figure 2, the curve for 1850 indicates a high degree of concentration in the ownership of real property.

The points plotted from the cumulative percentages of the population and of real estate values are next used to calculate the Gini index of concentration. This index is a measure of the area enclosed by the curve and the diagonal line as a percentage of the total area above the diagonal. It may range from .000 (perfect equality) to 1.000 (total concentration). The Gini index is used primarily for comparing degrees of concentration

[2]For a more detailed explanation of the Lorenz curve, see M. O. Lorenz, "Methods of Measuring the Concentration of Wealth," *Publications of the American Statistical Association* 9 (June, 1905), 209-219.

FIGURE 2

DISTRIBUTION OF REAL PROPERTY IN ANTEBELLUM TEXAS, 1850 AND 1860
(Lorenz Curve with Gini Index)

1850

Cumulative % of Population	34.5	45.2	56.6	70.6	92.8	96.9	99.1	99.8	100.0
Cumulative % of Property	0.0	1.1	3.7	9.9	39.1	56.7	74.9	87.1	100.0

Gini Index = .780

1860

Cumulative % of Population	33.1	37.3	45.8	58.7	88.4	93.9	97.5	99.4	100.0
Cumulative % of Property	0.0	0.2	1.3	4.5	27.2	39.8	57.4	77.6	100.0

Gini Index = .786

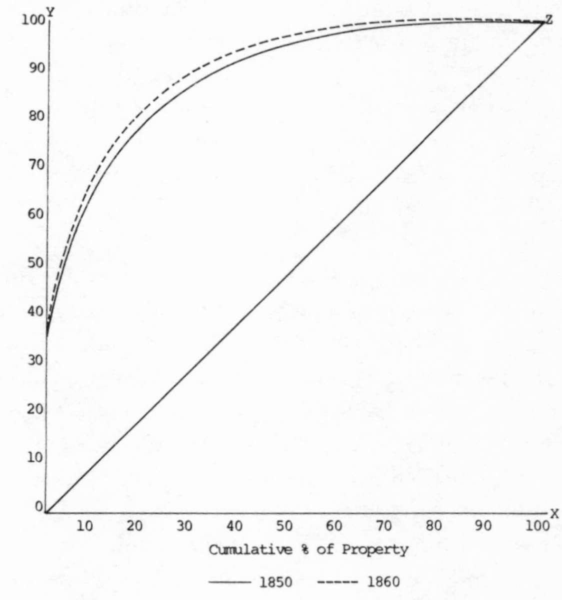

in one year or place or one category of wealth and property with those of another year or place or category.[3] The Gini does not automatically define a "high" or a "low" degree of concentration. This is a problem of interpretation that may be handled in two ways. First, the question of high and low may be determined simply in relation to the range of the statistic itself. Since the range of the Gini index is .000 to 1.000, it seems reasonable to interpret indices of .000 to .333 as indicators of a "low" level of concentration, those between .334 and .667 as representative of a "moderate" degree, and those of .668 or greater as measures of a "high" degree of concentration. Second, the question may be answered on the basis of comparisons of Gini indices for other times and places. In this case, a Gini of .750 may prove to be moderate or even low if the Ginis for other times and places are higher. In other words, the statistic may be regarded in either absolute or relative terms. We propose to interpret the Gini in absolute terms (i.e., on a scale relative to the statistic itself) until we reach chapter 8, which compares wealth concentrations in antebellum Texas with those for other places and times. There, a relative interpretation is called for.

One further caution about the Gini index is in order. Throughout this book dozens of comparisons of indices will be made, and in most cases the indices will differ less than .100. Although differences of this magnitude may not be significant, we nevertheless point them out in order to show patterns of differences from one region to another and from one census year to another. In short, small degrees of difference in individual cases may not be significant, but even in these cases, the patterns of differences should be noted.

In the case of real estate in 1850, the Gini index calculated for figure 2 is .780. The Lorenz curve for real estate in 1860 is very similar to that for 1850 and the index is .786. The calculation of these almost identical Gini indices for 1850 and 1860 demonstrates a high and virtually unchang-

[3]For a concise explanation of the Gini index, see Charles M. Dollar and Richard J. Jensen, *Historian's Guide to Statistics: Quantitative Analysis and Historical Research*, pp. 123-125.

ing degree of concentration in the ownership of real estate in antebellum Texas.

Before moving ahead to an analysis of the distribution of slave property in the 1850's, we must strongly emphasize that the Gini index, although a precise measure for purposes of comparison, rarely tells the whole story of economic inequality. A look at table 8 shows that the distributions of real property, from which virtually identical Gini indices were calculated, actually changed noticeably from 1850 to 1860. From one perspective, the wealthholding situation seemed to be improving for many people, since a smaller proportion of the family heads fell into the least wealthy group in the latter year. (The proportion who owned no real property barely changed, but those holding property worth less than $1,000 declined from 36.0 to 25.7 percent.) From a different perspective, however, there was an increase in the proportion of the largest real property holders and in their share of property in 1860. The group worth more than $10,000 (still less than 10 percent of the sample population) held 43.4 percent of all real property in 1850 but 60.2 percent by 1860. In the final analysis, these various shifts did not significantly alter the degree of concentration over the ten-year period. The decrease in the percentage of small property owners was matched by a sharp decline in their share of real property, and the increase in the proportion of wealthy owners was paralleled by an increase in their share of real property in a way that kept the Gini index of concentration at virtually the same level for both census years. Thus, for a complete picture of the wealthholding situation at any time, Gini indices must be used in conjunction with the distribution tables from which they were calculated.

Slave Property, 1850-1860

Slave property, as should be expected, was even more unequally distributed than real estate values among our sample populations for 1850 and 1860. Table 9 demonstrates that in 1850, 69.9 percent of the sample owned no slaves whereas the 6.6 percent who owned ten or more bondsmen controlled 61.8 percent of all slave property. Ten years later

TABLE 9

DISTRIBUTION OF SLAVE PROPERTY, 1850 AND 1860

1850

Number of Slaves	0	1-4	5-9	10-19	20-29	30-39	40-49	50-59	100+	Totals
% of Population	69.9	16.4	7.2	4.3	1.2	0.4	0.3	0.3	0.1	100.0
% of Slaves Held	0.0	15.8	22.4	26.3	13.3	6.6	5.4	8.0	2.2	100.0

1860

% of Population	72.7	13.0	6.5	4.8	1.4	0.7	0.4	0.4	0.1	100.0
% of Slaves Held	0.0	11.5	17.1	25.8	13.4	9.5	6.7	10.6	5.4	100.0

72.7 percent held no slaves and the 7.8 percent who owned ten or more slaves now controlled 71.4 percent of the total. Thus, there was a slight decline in the proportion of slaveholders in the population and a slight increase in the percentage of large holders. Slaveowners who had planter-size holdings of 20 or more bondsmen constituted only 2.3 percent of the population in 1850 and 3.0 percent in 1860, but they owned 35.5 percent of all slaves in 1850 and 45.6 percent ten years later. The Gini indices of concentration for slaveholding, .855 in 1850 and .876 in 1860, reveal a very high and relatively stable degree of inequality over the ten-year period.

It must be remembered that real estate values and slave property were the only two components of wealthholding among the entire population recorded in the censuses in both 1850 and 1860. Therefore, only the distributions of real and slave property may be compared directly as indicators of economic equality or inequality over the last decade of the antebellum period. In both cases, as we have seen, there were consistently high levels of concentration with the degree of inequality somewhat more pronounced in the holding of slave property. And in both cases, the trend from 1850 to 1860 was in favor of the largest holders of real and slave property. The investigation does not end at this point, however, because the census of 1860 included data on the value of personal as well as real estate. A distribution of personal property holdings according to these data is a further indication of the economic class structure existing in 1860, and a combination of real and personal estate values from the census of 1860 provides a comprehensive measure of wealthholding at the close of the antebellum period.

Personal Property and Wealth, 1860

Table 10 demonstrates that personal estate was far from equally distributed in 1860. Although only 9.7 percent of the sample population owned no personal property, the wealthiest 9.6 percent, those holding $10,000 or more, controlled 63.6 percent of the total value. The great majority of the sample (67.4 percent) had medium-sized holdings ranging from $250 to $9,999 in value, but their share of personal property was only 35.9 percent. There were fewer individuals in the sample for 1860

TABLE 10

DISTRIBUTION OF PERSONAL PROPERTY, 1860

$ Value of Personal Property	0	1-249	250-499	500-999	1,000-4,999	5,000-9,999	10,000-19,999	20,000-49,999	50,000+	Totals
% of Total Population	9.7	13.5	15.0	17.0	26.7	8.7	5.5	3.3	0.8	100.0
% of Personal Property	0.0	0.5	1.4	3.0	15.7	15.8	19.9	26.3	17.4	100.0

who owned no personal property than there were who held no real property. However, the degree of concentration for personal property, affected especially by the disproportionately small share held by those in the middle value range, was approximately the same (Gini index of .756) as for real estate (Gini index of .786). Obviously the combination of real and personal property held by each individual — a comprehensive measure of wealth in 1860 — produced a distribution similar to those already described for these two components. As table 11 demonstrates, only 8 percent of the sample held no form of wealth, 67.8 percent fell into the middle group who owned property worth $500 to $19,999, and wealthy holders of $20,000 or more constituted only 7.1 percent of the sample. (The dollar intervals for wealth are twice as large as those for real and personal property because wealth is a combination of these two forms of property.) This wealthiest 7.1 percent owned 56 percent of the wealth, leaving 44 percent as the share of the other 92.9 percent of the sample population. The Gini index for wealth, .742, indicates that there were no significant differences in the high degrees of concentration in the ownership of real estate, personal property, or a combination of the two in 1860.

Thus, every measure of wealthholding among the entire free population available from the censuses of 1850 and 1860 provides strong evidence that antebellum Texas was not a land of economic equality. Instead real estate, personal property, and slaves were concentrated in the hands

TABLE 11

DISTRIBUTION OF WEALTH, 1860

$ Value of Wealth	0	1-249	250-499	500-999	1,000-4,999	5,000-9,999	10,000-19,999	20,000-49,999	50,000+	Totals
% of Total Population	8.0	8.5	8.6	13.7	35.1	11.2	7.8	4.9	2.2	100.0
% of Wealth	0.0	0.2	0.5	1.5	12.5	12.2	17.2	23.8	32.2	100.0

of a minority of wealthy individuals. The degree of concentration in all categories increased very slightly from 1850 to 1860. Whether or not this wealthholding situation was unique in the antebellum United States is a question that will be dealt with in chapter 8.

The Regions of Antebellum Texas, 1850-1860

These generalizations apply to Texas as a whole in the 1850's, but the state, even the eastern two-fifths investigated by this study, was large enough to constitute practically a region of the antebellum South in itself. So the question now is whether the distributions of wealthholding were approximately the same for all geographic areas of Texas in 1850 and 1860, or whether there were significant differences in the degree of concentration in the ownership of property and slaves from the east Texas timberlands to the Gulf coastal plains to the north-central blackland prairies to the rolling hills of south-central Texas. The answer to this question should indicate whether wealth distributions were affected by such factors as time of settlement, proximity to coastal ports, prevalence of large plantations, frontier conditions, and others.

Region I, a relatively old and heavily settled east Texas area consisting of thirty-six upland counties covered with mixed forests, was characterized by a degree of inequality in wealthholding very comparable to that for the state as a whole in 1850 and 1860. The Gini indices presented in table 12 demonstrate this fact quite clearly. In the case of real estate, the indices for region I, .713 in 1850 and .735 in 1860, are only slightly lower than the statewide indices of .780 and .786. And the change in concentration in region I during the 1850's, although slight, was in the same direction — upward toward greater inequality in real property holdings — as for the whole state. Where slave property is concerned, the comparisons between region I and the state follow exactly the same patterns as in the case of real estate. Slaves were more concentrated than real property; region I had somewhat lower indices than the state as a whole; and the direction of change during the 1850's was toward greater inequality. In

TABLE 12

GINI INDICES: CONCENTRATION IN WEALTHHOLDING, 1850 AND 1860

	1850					1860				
	Whole State	Region I	Region II	Region III	Region IV	Whole State	Region I	Region II	Region III	Region IV
Real Property	.780	.713	.819	.750	.806	.786	.735	.816	.764	.793
Slaves	.855	.820	.877	.906	.856	.876	.841	.889	.892	.886
Personal Property	—	—	—	—	—	.756	.747	.824	.646	.774
Wealth	—	—	—	—	—	.742	.722	.791	.668	.753

1860 personal property and wealth in general were also slightly less concentrated in region I (indices of .747 and .722 respectively) than statewide (.756 and .742 respectively).

Thus, in region I there was a high and relatively stable degree of concentration in the ownership of real, personal, and slave property and total wealth during the 1850's, and levels of concentration there in 1850 and 1860 were quite comparable to those existing statewide. But as we have noted, relatively equal indices of concentration may be drawn from distributions varying greatly in the percentages of individuals holding small, medium, and large amounts of property. Therefore, a full investigation demands that we also examine the relative positions of region I's small, medium, and large holders of property and wealth in 1850 and 1860 and make comparisons with the relative positions of similar groups statewide.

This requirement, which of course extends to all categories of wealth in all four regions, poses a major problem in the presentation of data. Even if there were general similarities in the distributions of property, the relative positions of small, medium, and large holders were never precisely the same for any region compared with those for the whole state or for other regions. Significant regional variations in economic class structure, however much they may fit the same general pattern, must be described. The problem is one of detail.

We concluded that a detailed presentation with data tables for each indicator of wealthholding in all four regions would require too much space and too much tedious repetition of percentages for the same economic groups. The case of real property in region I may be taken as an example. The figures in table 13 compared with those in table 8 on the distribution of real property statewide demonstrate that the sample population of region I had a slightly smaller percentage of large holders than did the statewide sample, and that they in turn held a lesser share of real estate value. Only 1.9 percent of the regional sample owned real property valued at $10,000 or more in 1850 compared with 3.2 percent of the whole sample population who fell into this category. This wealthiest group in the regional sample held 26.1 percent of all real estate whereas the comparable group statewide owned 43.4 percent of the total. Ten years later region I's holders of $10,000 or more had increased to 4.6

TABLE 13

DISTRIBUTION OF REAL PROPERTY IN REGION I, 1850 AND 1860

1850

$ Value of Real Property	0	1-249	250-499	500-999	1,000-4,999	5,000-9,999	10,000-19,999	20,000-49,999	50,000+	Totals
% of Population	32.6	9.5	13.1	16.0	24.0	2.9	1.4	0.4	0.1	100.0
% of Real Property	0.0	1.4	4.1	9.7	42.3	16.4	16.1	8.0	2.0	100.0

1860

% of Population	28.8	4.2	9.6	14.2	32.3	6.3	3.3	1.1	0.2	100.0
% of Real Property	0.0	0.3	1.5	4.3	29.4	18.1	19.1	13.5	13.8	100.0

percent of the total (compared with 6.3 percent statewide), and they owned 46.4 percent of all real estate (compared with 60.2 percent). On the other hand, region I had a somewhat higher percentage of its population in the middle group (owners of $250-$9,999 in real estate) in both 1850 and 1860 (56 percent compared with 51.6 percent statewide in 1850 and 62.4 percent compared with 56.4 percent statewide in 1860), and this group held a larger share of the total real estate as well (72.5 percent to 55.5 percent statewide in 1850 and 53.3 percent to 39.6 percent statewide in 1860). Region I also had a slightly lower percentage of individuals in the poorest group (owners of less than $250 in real estate), and yet their share of real property was at least equal to that of the least wealthy group statewide.

In general then, the distribution of real estate in region I among small, medium, and large holders was very similar to that for the state as a whole. Large owners controlled a disproportionately large part of the real estate in region I in 1850 and 1860, there were noticeable increases in the percentage of large holders and their share of real property during the decade, the percentage of medium holders increased from 1850 to 1860 while their share of real estate declined, and so on. Nevertheless, it appears that members of the wealthiest group did not have quite the dominance in the control of real property in this east Texas area that they enjoyed in the state as a whole.

It should by now be obvious that detailed explanations of this sort for every indicator of wealthholding in all regions would be unreasonably cumbersome. Thus, the approach employed hereinafter will be to present the relevant Gini indices of concentration and then to generalize concerning the comparative positions of small, medium, and large holders in the various regions and their positions relative to similar groups statewide. All the data necessary to check the accuracy of these generalizations are provided in tabular form in appendix 1.

Turning from real estate to other indicators of wealthholding in region I, we again find overall patterns of distribution very similar to those in the state as a whole. The percentage of individuals owning slave property was higher in region I, however, and the increase in the percentages of large holders (owners of 20 or more bondsmen) and their share of slaves was greater there than it was statewide from 1850 to 1860. Small and medium holders in this east Texas area were slightly favored in 1850 by the fact that wealth in slaves was more widely held, but during the 1850's the planter class there advanced even more rapidly than it did statewide. Distributions of personal property and wealth in 1860 show no significant differences in the relative positions of small, medium, and large holders in region I and the state as a whole.

Region II, Gulf coastal Texas, consisting of thirteen coastal plain counties, was much less homogeneous than the east Texas area. Extending from the Louisiana border along the coast to Victoria and Calhoun counties near Corpus Christi, it included marshy small farming and grazing areas, the huge cotton and sugar plantation areas of Wharton, Fort Bend, Brazoria, and Matagorda counties, and two of the largest towns in antebellum Texas, Galveston and Houston. These circumstances combined to produce in region II the greatest degree of inequality in wealthholding found anywhere in Texas during the 1850's. As table 12 indicates, the indices of concentration for real estate, personal property, and wealth in region II, although not markedly greater, are higher in all cases in 1850 and 1860 than comparable indices for the state as a whole. In the case of real estate and slave property, the two indicators of wealthholding which reveal trends from 1850 to 1860, there was virtually no change during the decade.

Distributions of real, personal, and slave property and of wealth in general demonstrate that large wealthholders as a class were more important in region II than anywhere else in Texas. In every category of wealthholding in both 1850 and 1860, the richest class in region II constituted a larger percentage of the sample and held a much larger share of the property involved than did the wealthiest group statewide. The position of the richest class was primarily at the expense of the middle group, who generally held a much smaller share of property than did this group statewide. The percentage of individuals in the poorest class and their share of wealth were quite comparable in the samples for region II and for the whole state.

The thirty-two north-central prairie counties that made up region III were the most sparsely settled and rapidly growing area in antebellum Texas. Extending from the blackland prairies in the east to the 98th meridian in the west and from the Red River in the north well into central Texas near Austin, region III was certainly the most "frontier" area investigated in this study. And as might be expected, circumstances of wealthholding there varied noticeably from conditions statewide.

Variations in wealthholding for region III compared with the state as a whole are revealed in part, but only in part, by the Gini indices in table 12. Real estate was less concentrated in region III in 1850 and 1860, but the degree of difference was very slight and the trend was upward toward greater concentration. On the other hand, slave property was more concentrated in region III, but the trend there from 1850 to 1860, unlike the trend statewide, was very slightly downward. In 1860 the degree of concentration in personal property and wealth was markedly lower than the level of inequality statewide.

Region III's large wealthholders were a smaller group than the richest class statewide, and they held a lesser share of real, personal, and slave property and wealth in general. This was especially true in the case of slaveholding, where the richest class (holders of 20 or more slaves) constituted less than 1 percent of the population and held only about 20 percent of all slaves. At the same time, medium holders, those with real or personal property valued at $250 to $9,999, were a proportionately larger class owning a greater share of real and personal estate. In general, then, comparisons of the relative positions of small, medium, and large wealthholders in region III reveal a much smaller wealthy class there and a somewhat lower level of economic inequality. Only in the case of slaveholding was the degree of concentration greater than the degree statewide; that was because of the large percentage of non-slaveholders in this new region. Slaveholders constituted less than 20 percent of region III's population in both 1850 and 1860; therefore, slave property naturally was highly concentrated in the hands of a few individuals.

Region IV, consisting of twenty-four south-central Texas counties, shared features characteristic of each of the other three regions. Several of its eastern counties were geographically somewhat similar to the east Texas timberlands of region I. Washington and Colorado counties had cotton plantations to rival those further south on the Brazos and Colorado rivers in region II, whereas San Antonio and Austin (by 1860) provided urban areas also similar to those of region II. On its western border, region IV had sparsely settled areas much like the "frontier" of region III. This south-central region, perhaps because it shared features characteristic of the other regions, was in general most like the state as a whole in its patterns of wealthholding in 1850 and 1860.

The degree of concentration in real estate in region IV, although slightly higher than the level for the state as a whole in 1850, declined minutely during the decade and was virtually identical with the Gini index for real property statewide in 1860. Indices of concentration for slave property in region IV and the whole state were nearly equal for 1850 and 1860. Both personal property and wealth in total were slightly more concentrated in region IV than statewide, but the degree of difference was small.

Distributions of property do not, in this case, reveal any great divergences in the relative positions of small, medium, and large holders either. In the case of real estate, region IV's owners of property worth $10,000 or more were a somewhat larger group holding a greater percentage of all real estate value than the comparable group statewide in both 1850 and 1860. In the case of personal property, the poorest class, those holding less than $250 in value, was larger than statewide, and the middle group (owners of $250-$9,999 worth of personal estate) was smaller. But in both distributions the differences between region IV and the state as a whole were not great. A smaller percentage of slaves was held by planters in 1850, but by 1860 the percentage of slaveowners having twenty or more bondsmen in region IV and their share of all slave property was very comparable to the situation statewide.

Now that wealthholding in each region has been compared with the situation statewide in 1850 and 1860, it is necessary to offer some comparison, in less detail, of the various regions. Perhaps most striking in this connection is the relative uniformity of the high degree of concentration for all forms of wealth in all four regions. Every index of concentration presented in table 12 except that for personal property in region III in 1860 is greater than .667 on a scale of .000 to 1.000. And only one, that for slave property in region III in 1850, is greater than .900. Changes in the degree of concentration for real estate and slave property from 1850 to 1860 were very slight (no more than .030 in either direction) for all regions too. Thus levels of concentration were relatively uniform and unchanging. With this in mind, we may point out that region II, Gulf coastal Texas, had the greatest degree of inequality in all categories of wealthholding except slave property. In slaveholding, region II was a close second to region III, which presented a high Gini index primarily because it had so few slaveholders. Region I, on the other hand, had the lowest level of concentration in real and slave property in 1850 and 1860, whereas region III had the lowest levels in personal property and total wealth in 1860.

An examination of the relative positions of small, medium, and large wealthholders reveals that region II consistently had a larger proportion of its population in the wealthiest group, whereas region III, the more frontier area of north-central Texas, generally had the smallest percentage of large holders. The distributions of small and medium wealthholders defy any generalization that will hold for all four regions. Region I, for example, had a larger proportion of medium-range real property holders than did the other regions in 1850 and 1860, but in the case of personal property and wealth in 1860, this region did not have the largest group of medium holders. Other attempts to find significant patterns of comparison for small and medium holders across the regions fail similarly.

Summary

In conclusion, an analysis of wealthholding among the entire free population, rather than of the farming population alone as in previous studies by Phillips, Gray, Owsley, and Wright, reveals a high degree of inequality among antebellum Texans.[4] Real property, personal property, slaves, and total wealth were concentrated under the control of a small minority (less than 10 percent of the total population). Distributions of these indicators of wealthholding reveal an increase from 1850 to 1860 in the percentage of individuals in the wealthiest group and in their share of real property and slaves. On the other hand, the degree of concentration in the ownership of real estate and slaves increased only slightly; certainly there was no sharp rise in the level of economic inequality in the last antebellum decade.

There was some variation in the degree of economic inequality from region to region in antebellum Texas, but the differences in levels of concentration are not so striking as the similarities. Basically, the high degree of concentration in wealthholding extended across all regions of antebellum Texas with remarkable uniformity and stability from 1850 to 1860. Even in the more western frontier area of north-central Texas (region III) indices of concentration were comparable to those elsewhere in the state. On the other hand, the distributions of large, medium, and small wealthholders do indicate some notable variations from region to region. Region III had proportionately fewer large property holders and fewer slaveholders than the others. The absence of a numerous class of very wealthy families may have created a feeling that economic equality existed on this frontier. Certainly, the family with small or medium-sized holdings saw much more of people like themselves in their everyday existence than they saw of the elite slaveholding class. By contrast, families with small or medium holdings in region II saw a great deal of this elite group. In some coastal counties they were surrounded by huge plantations with large slave forces, constant reminders of existing economic inequality. The other two regions (I and IV) more nearly approxi-

[4]One possible objection to the methods employed in this chapter lies in the consideration of wealthholding among the free population alone rather than among the entire population (i.e., slave as well as free). It may be objected that this approach treats slaves as property rather than as human beings and therefore misrepresents the actual distribution of wealth in antebellum Texas. For a full discussion of this matter, see appendix 2.

mated the statewide situation both in levels of concentration and in distributions of large, medium, and small property holders.

These conclusions certainly suggest that the planter-dominance thesis is a more accurate description of antebellum Texas than the yeoman-democracy interpretation. However, since the original historiographical debate centered on the farm population rather than on the whole free population — as indeed the terms *planter-dominance* and *yeoman-democracy* indicate — we must eventually consider Texas' agricultural population alone for the purpose of more precise comparisons with previous work. But first, wealthholding among the general population must be analyzed further in terms of the characteristics of individual wealthholders.

Chapter 4.

Some Characteristics of Wealthholders

ANALYSIS and comparisons of wealthholdings to this point have been made on the basis of the proportions of the population falling into economic groups and the percentages of the various forms of wealth that they held. This is the most valid way to compare the distributions of wealth in sample populations drawn from an area as large as antebellum Texas and separated by a period of ten years. This approach, however, though very descriptive concerning concentration in wealthholding, does not reveal much about the characteristics of individual wealthholders, a related but distinct question. Did individual characteristics such as age and place of birth affect wealthholding? How did an individual's occupational and slaveholding status relate to his economic circumstances? The purpose of this chapter, then, is to consider these characteristics as determinants of differences in wealthholding among heads of families in antebellum Texas.

Table 14 reveals that wealthholding status was in general positively related to increasing age. Heads of households in the youngest age group (those under twenty years of age) had mean wealthholdings only 10 percent as large as those of family heads aged fifty-five to sixty-four. Moreover, mean wealth increased at each age level up to age sixty-five and over.

Wealthholding was also affected by foreign as opposed to American birth and, to a lesser extent, by where an individual was born within the United States. As table 15 indicates, the foreign-born were less than half as wealthy on the average as were natives of the United States. Among the native-born, individuals from the free states had mean wealthholdings

TABLE 14

MEAN VALUE OF WEALTH ACCORDING TO AGE

TEXAS, 1860

Age	0-19	20-29	30-34	35-39	40-44	45-54	55-64	65+
Wealth	$1,157.35	$3,090.80	$4,392.67	$5,886.81	$7,297.16	$9,341.82	$11,348.52	$9,631.76

roughly 85 percent as large as those of Southerners. Thus, Northerners were considerably richer than foreigners but slightly less wealthy than Southerners. Natives of the lower South were on the average the wealthiest of all the birthplace groups.

Not too surprisingly, wealthholding differences were clearly related to the occupation and the slaveholding status of the individual. Table 16 demonstrates that overseers and skilled and unskilled workers, the least wealthy occupational groups, were less than 10 percent as rich as those who engaged in various forms of commerce (primarily merchants). Ranking below the commercial group in descending order were professionals (such as lawyers and physicians), public officials (such as judges and sheriffs), farmers, manufacturers, skilled tradesmen (such as blacksmiths and carpenters), unskilled workers (such as common laborers), and finally, overseers.[1] As expected, slaveholders, whose mean wealth was $18,370, were far richer than non-slaveholders, who averaged $1,907 in total wealth (see table 23).

Of the four characteristics discussed above — age, birthplace, occupation, and slaveholding — the last is such an obvious determinant of wealthholding status that further analysis seems unnecessary. In the case of the other three, however, some interesting patterns emerge.

[1]Our analysis of the impact of occupation on wealthholding depends on the occupation as given by the respondent to the census enumerator. As mentioned earlier, someone who called himself a lawyer or merchant may have been a farmer also. Thus, in a few cases individuals classed with one occupation group for wealthholding analysis may have actually belonged to more than one occupation group.

TABLE 15

MEAN VALUE OF WEALTH ACCORDING TO PLACE OF BIRTH

TEXAS, 1860

Birthplace	Lower South	Upper South	Free States	Foreign-Born	Unknown
Wealth	$7,329.75	$6,926.25	$6,092.76	$2,811.01	$1,781.80

TABLE 16

MEAN VALUE OF WEALTH ACCORDING TO OCCUPATION

TEXAS, 1860

Occupation	Farming	Commerce	Professions	Public Office	Manufacturing	Skilled Trades	Unskilled Services	Overseer
Wealth	$6,894.72	$14,896.59	$9,234.85	$7,303.46	$4,735.14	$1,485.52	$1,160.44	$ 671.42

The positive relationship between increasing age and improving wealthholding status (table 14) indicates that many antebellum Texans participated to some extent in the "American Dream." As the years passed and individuals accumulated wealth through savings and inheritance, their economic status noticeably improved. This did not necessarily mean that the "egalitarian ideal" was becoming reality (great variations in wealthholding still existed), only that most individuals did become wealthier as they became older.

Since age was obviously important in explaining wealth differentials, could it be that age also explained the varying economic statuses of different birthplace groups? For example, did youth explain the fact that (as shown in table 15) the foreign-born were poorer than others? A glance at table 17 indicates that the answer is no. Foreigners did not differ significantly in age from the other birthplace groups. The explanation of their

TABLE 17

MEAN AGES OF HEADS OF HOUSEHOLDS ACCORDING TO PLACE OF BIRTH

TEXAS, 1860

Place of Birth	Lower South	Upper South	Free States	Foreign Born	Unknown	Total Sample
Mean Age	37.2	41.0	38.1	38.5	37.7	39.0

lower wealth status must lie elsewhere. Their lack of economic resources upon arrival in Texas, their unfamiliarity with the language, customs, and laws of the state, and their concentration in relatively low-paying skilled and unskilled service occupations probably explain their poorer economic circumstances.

Another method of examining the characteristics of wealthholders in antebellum Texas is to arrange family heads into three wealth classes and to observe the similarities and differences in these characteristics from one class to the next. To this purpose, the sample population must be divided into a poorest class (those having total wealth of less than $500), a middle class (those with wealthholdings of $500 to $19,999), and a wealthiest class (individuals worth $20,000 or more). Were there, as one would expect from previous analysis in this chapter, noticeable differences among these three groups in terms of age, birthplace, occupation, and slaveholding?

Table 18 provides further evidence that wealth was positively related to age. Whereas household heads under the age of thirty-five made up 40.7 percent of the total sample, they were a majority (59.2 percent) of the poorest wealth group and only 17.1 percent of the richest class. In short, the young were overrepresented among the poor and underrepresented among the wealthy. By contrast, older family heads (forty-five years old or older) were underrepresented in the least wealthy class and overrepresented in the richest.

In general, table 19 bears out the relationships between birthplace

TABLE 18

DISTRIBUTION OF WEALTHHOLDERS ACCORDING TO AGE AND WEALTH CLASS, TEXAS, 1860

(In Percentages)

Age	$0 - 499	$500 - 19,999	$20,000 and over	Total Sample Population
0 - 19	1.0	0.1	0.0	0.4
20 - 29	38.1	19.2	7.7	23.1
30 - 34	20.1	17.0	9.4	17.2
35 - 39	13.2	16.7	12.3	15.5
40 - 44	9.2	14.2	18.3	13.2
45 - 54	11.8	21.0	31.4	19.4
55 - 64	5.2	9.1	16.6	8.7
65 and over	1.4	2.7	4.3	2.5
Total	100.0	100.0	100.0	100.0

TABLE 19

DISTRIBUTION OF WEALTHHOLDERS ACCORDING TO PLACE OF BIRTH AND WEALTH CLASS, TEXAS, 1860

(In Percentages)

	$0-499	$500-19,999	$20,000 and over	Total Sample Population
Lower South*	36.2	35.2	42.6	36.0
Upper South**	31.8	44.1	45.7	41.1
Free States	8.3	8.2	7.1	8.1
Foreign-Born	23.3	12.2	4.6	14.5
Unknown	0.4	0.3	0.0	0.3
Totals	100.0	100.0	100.0	100.0

* Alabama, Arkansas, Florida, Georgia, Louisiana, Mississippi, South Carolina, Texas

** North Carolina, Virginia, Kentucky, Maryland, Tennessee, Delaware, Missouri, District of Columbia

and wealthholding revealed in our analysis of mean wealthholding according to nativity. Most striking, the foreign-born were overrepresented among the least wealthy and even more clearly underrepresented in the richest class. For the other nativity groups, there was roughly proportional representation among the three wealth groups. The only notable exception was in the case of upper Southerners, who were underrepresented in the poorest class.

Table 20 demonstrates the problems of analyzing the relationship of occupation to wealthholding when more than two-thirds of the sample engage in the same kind of work, in this case farming. Although they were somewhat underrepresented in the poorest group and overrepresented in the other two, farmers constituted a majority of each wealth class. As expected, skilled and unskilled laborers were overrepresented among the poor and greatly underrepresented among the rich. Those who were engaged in commerce and the professions, on the other hand, demonstrated the opposite pattern. Virtually every individual in the poorest group was a non-slaveholder, and nearly all in the wealthiest class were owners of bondsmen (see table 21).

One final method of describing the characteristics of wealthholders is to examine the range of wealth differences from one class to another. Table 22, which summarizes wealthholdings per household head in 1860, demonstrates that this range was great indeed. Whereas individual family heads in the poorest class averaged only $168 in wealth, those in the middle class had mean holdings of $4,091, and the wealthiest class averaged $50,294 per family head. Those in the upper class were on the average nearly 300 times richer than those in the lower group.[2] Among the four regions of Texas, the Gulf coastal area (region II) displayed the greatest variation from the statewide means. There the poor were poorer and the rich were richer than elsewhere in the state.

Disparities in wealthholding were also striking when consideration is shifted from the three wealth groups to slaveholders and non-slave-

[2]As revealed in table 11 of chapter 3, 25.1 percent of the sample households fell in the lower wealth class, 67.8 percent in the middle group, and 7.1 percent in the richest class.

TABLE 20

DISTRIBUTION OF WEALTHHOLDERS ACCORDING TO OCCUPATION AND WEALTH CLASS, TEXAS, 1860

(In Percentages)

	Holders of $0-499	Holders of $500-19,999	Holders of $20,000 and over	Total Sample Population
Farming	50.9	75.0	76.0	69.0
Commerce	2.3	4.4	11.4	4.3
Professions	3.1	5.3	8.9	5.0
Public Office	0.8	0.8	1.1	0.8
Manufacturing	1.4	1.1	0.6	1.2
Skilled Trades	14.8	7.9	0.3	9.1
Unskilled Services	24.1	4.5	0.6	9.2
Overseer	1.9	0.4	0.0	0.7
Miscellaneous	0.7	0.6	1.1	0.7
Totals	100.0	100.0	100.0	100.0

TABLE 21

DISTRIBUTION OF WEALTHHOLDERS ACCORDING TO SLAVEHOLDING STATUS AND WEALTH CLASS, TEXAS, 1860

(In Percentages)

	$0-499	$500-19,999	$20,000-and over	Total Sample Population
Slaveholders	0.3	30.3	93.4	27.3
Non-Slaveholders	99.7	69.7	6.6	72.7
Totals	100.0	100.0	100.0	100.0

holders. Table 23 indicates that the average slaveholder was far richer than his non-slaveholding counterpart. Slaveowners averaged nearly ten times as much wealth as non-slaveholders statewide, and the same pattern held true in the four regions of Texas. It might be argued that the

TABLE 22

MEAN VALUE OF WEALTH PER HEAD OF HOUSEHOLD ACCORDING TO WEALTH CLASS

1860

	$0 - 499	$500 - 19,999	$20,000 and over
Texas	$168	$4,091	$50,294
Region I	203	4,354	46,775
Region II	85	4,337	67,842
Region III	207	3,630	44,526
Region IV	119	4,180	45,953

TABLE 23

MEAN VALUE OF WEALTH AND REAL PROPERTY:

SLAVEHOLDERS AND NON-SLAVEHOLDERS, 1860

	Wealth		Real Property	
	Slaveholders	Non-Slaveholders	Slaveholders	Non-Slaveholders
Texas	$18,370	$1,907	$ 7,369	$ 950
Region I	16,198	1,452	5,221	679
Region II	34,907	3,716	18,001	2,196
Region III	13,077	1,888	5,985	875
Region IV	20,969	1,916	8,813	974

ownership of slave property automatically made slaveholders far wealthier than non-slaveholders. Table 23 also reveals, however, that when calculations are limited to real property alone (i.e., slaves and all other forms of personal property are excluded from consideration), slaveowners were still roughly eight times as rich on the average as non-slaveholders. Certainly, slaveowners held large amounts of real property partly because they also owned slaves, but it is worth noting that it was not the value of their slaves alone that made them wealthy.

In summary, wealthholders in the poorest class shared the following characteristics: they had mean wealthholdings a great deal smaller (300 times smaller in actual dollar value) than those of the richest class; they were almost invariably non-slaveowners; they were more likely to be foreign-born than were individuals in the middle and upper classes; they were generally younger (in their twenties and thirties); and an unusually large number of them were tradesmen or laborers. By contrast, family heads in the richest class had wealthholdings vastly larger in actual dollar value than those in the poorest and middle groups. All but a few in the upper class were slaveowners, and nearly 90 percent of these wealthy Texans were natives of the South (compared with 77.1 percent statewide). A majority were forty-five years of age or older, and virtually all were engaged in farming, commerce, or the professions. Heads of households in the middle wealthholding class conformed closely to the pattern of the population as a whole in terms of slaveholding, birthplace, age, and occupation.

The foregoing characterization of classes of wealthholders should not be taken as an attempt to explain totally why disparities in wealthholding (and therefore concentration of wealth) existed in antebellum Texas. There are at least as many reasons for disparities in wealthholding as there are individuals in society. Not even brothers normally share the same degree of intelligence, industriousness, opportunity, and luck. Thus, the "why" of wealth differentials and concentration becomes a very difficult question to answer with finality. Our purpose has been to indicate that individuals within each of the three wealth classes tended to share certain characteristics with each other. This cannot completely explain why individuals fell into particular classes or why there was a particular level of wealth concentration, but it does suggest some of the factors that determined the economic status of antebellum Texans.

Chapter 5.

Distribution of Agricultural Property and Production, 1850-1860

THE investigation of wealthholding and economic class structure in antebellum Texas does not end with an analysis of the distributions of real estate, slave property, personal property, and total wealth. These are the only indicators of wealthholding that apply to the entire free population, but a full examination of economic equality and/or inequality requires analysis of the distributions of important agricultural property and products as well. In fact, as explained earlier, previous work on economic and social arrangements in the antebellum South has focused on agricultural wealthholding alone. Moreover, in a primarily agricultural area like antebellum Texas, the degree of concentration in crop-producing acreage or in the key staple crop of cotton, for example, is very revealing of economic structure in general. Finally, measurements of concentration in agricultural property and production may suggest more about the distribution of income than do similar measurements for real and personal property holdings.

It is a simple matter to demonstrate that Texas in the 1850's was overwhelmingly agricultural. As we explained in chapter 2, approximately three-quarters of both our sample populations (77.5 percent in 1850 and 74.4 percent in 1860) were directly involved in agriculture, either as farmers by occupation or as owners of farm property even if they had another occupation. (These figures do not refer simply to those who listed their occupation as "farmer" in the census, but also to those with other occupations who owned farm acreage. Therefore, the percentages given here for the agricultural population are somewhat higher than those presented in table 3, which are given according to the primary occupation recorded in the census.) These agricultural populations for 1850 and 1860 were easily subdivided into four groups according to slaveholding and landholding status. Individuals who owned farm acreage were located in Schedule IV, and those who held slaves also appeared in Schedule II. Table 24 demonstrates that in both 1850 and 1860 slaveholders constituted only one-third of the state's agricultural population; the other two-thirds were non-slaveholders. There were, however, very few slave-holding farmers who did not own land. On the other hand, a sizable proportion of the non-slaveholders were also non-landholders. Overall, the percentage of landless farmers in Texas, that is, those who held

TABLE 24

DISTRIBUTION OF FARMERS ACCORDING TO SLAVEHOLDING AND LANDHOLDING STATUS, TEXAS, 1850 AND 1860

(In Percentages)

1850

	Whole State	Region I	Region II	Region III	Region IV
Slaveholding Farmers with Farms	30.7	32.6	44.1	18.0	32.4
Slaveholding Farmers without Farms	2.7	4.0	2.1	0.4	1.6
Non-Slaveholding Farmers with Farms	50.2	45.6	36.5	68.5	50.6
Non-Slaveholding Farmers without Farms	16.4	17.8	17.3	13.1	15.3
Totals	100.0	100.0	100.0	100.0	100.0

1860

	Whole State	Region I	Region II	Region III	Region IV
Slaveholding Farmers with Farms	30.5	36.4	52.4	20.4	29.5
Slaveholding Farmers without Farms	1.7	1.6	3.4	1.8	1.6
Non-Slaveholding Farmers with Farms	50.3	47.8	36.2	53.8	52.6
Non-Slaveholding Farmers without Farms	17.5	14.2	8.0	24.0	16.3
Totals	100.0	100.0	100.0	100.0	100.0

neither improved nor unimproved acreage, was remarkably stable at 19.1 percent of the sample agricultural population in 1850 and 19.2 percent in 1860.[1]

Before we move into an examination of the distribution of agricultural property and production, attention should be given briefly to the degree of concentration in general wealthholding among the farm population. Table 25, when compared with table 12 in chapter 3, demonstrates that Gini indices for real estate, personal property, slaves, and total wealth were slightly lower for the farm population (statewide and in each region) than for the population as a whole. This circumstance is explained primarily by the elimination of non-farming non-slaveholders (many of whom held little wealth) from the calculation when only the agricultural population is considered.[2] Nevertheless, the degree of concentration in wealthholding among farmers was almost invariably high (indices were between .667 and .900 in almost every case) and relatively stable from 1850 to 1860.

The data on wealth indicators such as real property and slaves are found in Schedules I and II of the census returns; further statistical information on the agricultural population, at least on those who owned land, is found in Schedule IV, which reported in detail on the size, value, and production of each farm. Although census enumerators recorded everything from the number of improved acres to the pounds of honey and beeswax produced, it is obvious that only a few items, such as cotton

[1]Frank Lawrence Owsley, *Plain Folk of the Old South*, p. 16, contends that except for the Carolinas and Virginia, which he had not examined, approximately 80 to 85 percent of the agricultural population owned their land. Our findings for Texas support this general estimate. However, Owsley found an increase in the percentage of landholding farmers from 1850 to 1860 in many of his sample counties in Alabama, Mississippi, Tennessee, Georgia, and Louisiana (chapter 5 of *Plain Folk*); we did not find this true for Texas.

[2]Gavin Wright, " 'Economic Democracy' and the Concentration of Agricultural Wealth in the Cotton South, 1850-1860," *Agricultural History* 44 (January, 1970), 69, suggested that a comparison of wealth concentrations among the entire free population and the farming population alone would reveal a greater degree of economic equality among the latter. Our investigation confirms this suggestion.

TABLE 25

GINI INDICES: PROPERTY AND PRODUCTION OF AGRICULTURAL POPULATION, 1850 AND 1860

1850

	Whole State	Region I	Region II	Region III	Region IV
Real Property	.762	.705	.794	.740	.757
Slave Property	.842	.814	.827	.902	.810
Personal Property	---	---	---	---	---
Wealth	---	---	---	---	---
Improved Acreage	.597	.596	.724	.454	.598
Cash Value of Farm	.685	.650	.736	.638	.688
Livestock	.615	.566	.678	.516	.601
Corn	.658	.636	.786	.628	.616
Cotton	.906	.864	.929	.956	.877

1860

	Whole State	Region I	Region II	Region III	Region IV
Real Property	.747	.680	.738	.749	.747
Slave Property	.854	.823	.773	.882	.853
Personal Property	.729	.733	.706	.632	.730
Wealth	.710	.695	.681	.654	.707
Improved Acreage	.635	.588	.702	.623	.662
Cash Value of Farm	.713	.610	.747	.734	.725
Livestock	.647	.580	.655	.649	.657
Corn	.694	.609	.720	.711	.747
Cotton	.880	.811	.865	.969	.851

production, have much significance for the questions of economic structure in general. Therefore, this chapter will focus on the five categories of agricultural property and production we consider most relevant to our investigation: number of improved acres, cash value of farm, dollar value of livestock, number of bushels of corn, and number of bales of cotton. Other potential cash crops, such as sugar, tobacco, and rice, were too small or too regional to be of use in a statewide study.

Improved Acreage, 1850-1860

Improved acreage was defined for the census enumerators as land "cleared and used for grazing, grass, or tillage, or which is now fallow, connected with or belonging to the farm . . . ."[3] Although this definition may seem broad, the amount of improved acreage held by each farmer was a good indicator of his economic status, for it reveals the amount of land immediately available for production. Furthermore, it seems that census enumerators and respondents sought accuracy in the figures they reported. They did not, for example, consistently report improved acreage in round numbers. And they did regularly record, especially in western areas, a number of improved and unimproved acres totaling a section (640 acres) or some fraction thereof.

The Gini indices of concentration presented in table 25 demonstrate a moderately high and stable degree of inequality in the distribution of improved acreage among our sample agricultural populations in 1850 (.597) and 1860 (.635). Looking behind these indices of concentration to the relative positions of small, medium, and large farmers (table 26), we find that a small group of large holders of improved acreage, those having 300 or more acres, enjoyed a considerable advantage over other farmers. This group, which constituted only 1 percent of the total agricultural population in 1850 and 3.2 percent ten years later, held 14.7 percent of all improved acreage in 1850 and 28.1 percent in 1860. The percentage of medium holders (those owning 50 to 299 acres) increased almost ten points, but their share of the total improved acreage did not advance. Although small holders (0 to 49 acres) decreased as a group, their percentage of improved acreage declined even more rapidly. There was a slight reduction during the decade in the percentage of farmers without improved acreage, but approximately one-quarter of the farming population in both 1850 and 1860 held none.[4]

Slaveholding farmers enjoyed a clear-cut superiority over non-slaveholding farmers in the ownership of improved acreage. Although they decreased slightly as a proportion of the agricultural population during the 1850's, from 33.4 percent to 32.1 percent of the total, slaveholders'

[3]Carroll D. Wright, *The History and Growth of the United States Census*, p. 235.

[4]A farmer without *improved* acreage is not necessarily a landless farmer. He may have held unimproved acreage.

TABLE 26

DISTRIBUTION OF IMPROVED ACREAGE, TEXAS, 1850 AND 1860

1850

No. of Improved Acres	0	1-49	50-99	100-199	200-299	300-399	400-499	500-999	1,000+	Totals
% of Farm Population	26.2	53.9	12.1	5.4	1.4	0.5	0.1	0.3	0.1	100.0
% of Improved Acres	0.0	33.5	22.8	19.9	9.1	5.0	1.3	5.9	2.5	100.0
% of Slaveholding Farmers	4.2	13.6	8.3	5.0	1.3	0.5	0.1	0.3	0.1	33.4
% of Improved Acres	0.0	10.4	15.9	18.4	8.8	5.0	1.3	5.9	2.5	68.2
% of Non-Slaveholding Farmers	22.0	40.3	3.8	0.4	0.1	0.0	0.0	0.0	0.0	66.6
% of Improved Acres	0.0	23.1	6.9	1.5	0.3	0.0	0.0	0.0	0.0	31.8

1860

No. of Improved Acres	0	1-49	50-99	100-199	200-299	300-399	400-499	500-999	1,000+	Totals
% of Farm Population	23.3	45.5	16.0	9.1	2.9	1.3	0.8	1.0	0.1	100.0
% of Improved Acres	0.0	19.8	19.3	21.0	11.7	7.9	6.1	11.3	2.8	99.9
% of Slaveholding Farmers	2.4	7.8	8.6	7.7	2.7	1.2	0.7	0.9	0.1	32.1
% of Improved Acres	0.0	4.1	10.9	17.9	10.8	7.6	5.9	11.0	2.8	71.0
% of Non-Slaveholding Farmers	20.9	37.7	7.4	1.4	0.2	0.1	0.1	0.1	0.0	67.9
% of Improved Acres	0.0	15.7	8.4	3.1	0.9	0.3	0.2	0.3	0.0	28.9

share of all improved acreage actually increased from 68.2 percent to 71 percent. In both 1850 and 1860 slaveholders were only a small fraction of the farmers without improved acreage while constituting virtually all the holders of 300 or more acres.

In summary, then, there was a moderately high degree of concentration in the distribution of improved acreage among Texas farmers in 1850, and the level of inequality increased slightly during the next ten years. Farmers with medium holdings increased as a percentage of the farming population during the 1850's, but there was no concomitant increase in their share of improved land. The small group of large farmers consistently held a disproportionately large share of improved acreage. Slaveholding farmers, although only a third of the agricultural population, enjoyed control of more than two-thirds of this most important form of property.

Cash Value of Farm, 1850-1860

The third item recorded for each farm reported in Schedule IV, following improved acreage and unimproved acreage, was called "cash value of farm." Under this heading census enumerators were instructed to list "the actual cash value of the whole number of acres returned by you as improved and unimproved." This figure was to include the value of buildings and improvements, but it did not encompass the value of livestock, farm implements, or any type of personal property. Thus, the cash-value-of-farm figures offer some measurement of the quality of land held by each farmer, the conditions of fences and outbuildings, and the comfort of the family house. And so it may be argued that this census item provides an even better indicator of an individual farmer's economic status than the number of improved acres he owned.[5]

Farm value was noticeably more concentrated than improved acreage in both 1850 and 1860 (see table 25). The Gini index for cash value

[5]The census taker's instructions are in Carroll D. Wright, *History and Growth of the United States Census*, pp. 235-236. Gavin Wright, " 'Economic Democracy' and Agricultural Wealth," p. 75, assumes that the cash-value-of-farm figure includes the value of buildings and improvements on the land. This assumption seems reasonable to us.

across the state was high (.685) in 1850, and it increased slightly (to .713) by 1860. The relative stability of these indices is very similar to the situation for improved acreage, but the fact that they are higher indicates that the degree of economic inequality among the agricultural population was even greater than the distribution of improved acreage suggests. How did this higher level of concentration in farm value show up in the relative positions of small, medium, and large farmers?

Table 27 demonstrates that from 1850 to 1860 the group who owned farms worth $10,000 or more increased from 1 percent to 4.9 percent of the agricultural population while their share of the total cash value of farms advanced from 17.5 to 47.3 percent. In the same period, owners of farms having small (0 to $249) or medium-range ($250 to $9,999) cash values saw the total value of their farm property decline as a proportion of the total. As we have seen, the distribution of improved acreage among small, medium, and large farmers in 1850 and 1860 followed this same general pattern. But by 1860, the percentage of farmers holding land worth $10,000 or more (4.9 percent) was greater than and increasing more rapidly than the percentage of large farmers holding 300 or more improved acres (3.2 percent), and the proportion of all cash value represented by the most valuable farms (47.3 percent) was much greater than and increasing more rapidly than the share of improved acreage held by the largest farmers (28.1 percent). This circumstance suggests that the small group of large farmers not only held a disproportionate share of improved acreage, but that by 1860 the land they owned was more valuable and enhanced by more improvements and better houses. The great majority of large farmers were, of course, slaveholders, so the owners of bondsmen controlled virtually all the most valuable farms and held a very large share of farm value in general. By 1860, for example, slaveholding farmers, although just less than one-third of the agricultural population, held almost three-quarters of the cash value of all farms.

Value of Livestock, 1850-1860

Schedule IV of the census reported extensive information concerning

TABLE 27

DISTRIBUTION OF CASH VALUE OF FARMS, TEXAS, 1850 AND 1860

1850

$ of Cash Value	0	1-249	250-499	500-999	1,000-4,999	5,000-9,999	10,000-19,999	20,000-49,999	50,000+	Totals
% of Farm Population	26.7	14.8	14.6	17.8	22.6	2.5	0.7	0.2	0.1	100.0
% of Cash Value	0.0	2.2	5.3	12.5	45.7	16.8	9.2	6.2	2.1	100.0
% of Slaveholding Farmers	4.3	2.1	3.4	6.3	14.3	2.1	0.6	0.2	0.1	33.4
% of Cash Value	0.0	0.3	1.3	4.5	30.5	13.9	8.5	6.2	2.1	67.3
% of Non-Slaveholding Farmers	22.4	12.7	11.2	11.5	8.3	0.4	0.1	0.0	0.0	66.6
% of Cash Value	0.0	1.9	4.0	8.0	15.2	2.9	0.7	0.0	0.0	32.7

1860

$ of Cash Value	0	1-249	250-499	500-999	1,000-4,999	5,000-9,999	10,000-19,999	20,000-49,999	50,000+	Totals
% of Farm Population	23.3	6.3	10.2	15.9	34.4	5.0	3.2	1.3	0.4	100.0
% of Cash Value	0.0	0.4	1.6	4.8	31.8	14.1	18.1	17.0	12.2	100.0
% of Slaveholding Farmers	2.5	0.7	1.4	2.7	16.2	4.3	2.8	1.2	0.4	32.2
% of Cash Value	0.0	0.1	0.2	0.9	16.9	12.3	15.4	16.2	12.2	74.2
% of Non-Slaveholding Farmers	20.8	5.6	8.8	13.2	18.2	0.7	0.4	0.1	0.0	67.8
% of Cash Value	0.0	0.3	1.4	3.9	14.9	1.8	2.7	0.8	0.0	25.8

each farm's livestock. The enumerators recorded the number of animals of each type and an estimate of the total cash value of all livestock. At least 80 percent of our sample farms reported some figure for livestock value. And although antebellum Texas was by no means a ranching area, several western counties in our study had a few farms that were engaged primarily in cattle raising. Certainly then, the value of a farm's livestock may be considered as an indicator of economic status among the agricultural population in general.

Table 25 demonstrates that the degree of concentration for livestock value was somewhat lower than that for cash value of farm but very comparable to that for ownership of improved acreage. During the 1850's, the livestock holdings of small (less than $250 in livestock value) and medium farmers ($250 to $1,999) declined relative to the share owned by those who reported $2,000 or more in livestock value (see table 28). Those with large holdings of livestock increased very rapidly during the 1850's, from 4.1 percent to 12.3 percent; in fact they increased much more rapidly than did their proportion of livestock value. Nevertheless, this relatively small group held 55.2 percent of the cash value of livestock in 1860.

Interestingly enough, slaveholding farmers did not enjoy quite the advantage in controlling livestock value that they had in other categories of agricultural property and production. Although disproportionately large, the slaveholders' share of livestock value (approximately 60 percent in 1850 and 1860) was noticeably less than their share of improved acreage, cash value of farms, corn, or cotton. Few slaveholding farmers had no livestock, but unlike the situation in improved acreage and cash value, the wealthiest group of livestock owners was not composed almost entirely of slaveholders.

Corn Production, 1850-1860

Corn was the most important general farm crop in antebellum Texas. Certainly it was the most universally cultivated grain. The agricultural returns for 1850 and 1860 show that corn production greatly exceeded the

TABLE 28

DISTRIBUTION OF LIVESTOCK BY VALUE, TEXAS, 1850 AND 1860

1850

$ Value of Livestock	0	1-99	100-249	250-499	500-999	1,000-1,499	1,500-1,999	2,000-4,999	5,000+	Totals
% of Farm Population	19.4	4.8	20.6	23.3	18.4	6.8	2.6	3.3	0.8	100.0
% of Livestock Value	0.0	0.5	6.6	15.4	23.6	15.0	8.2	17.8	12.9	100.0
% of Slaveholding Farmers	2.7	0.5	3.6	7.7	9.4	4.3	1.7	2.8	0.7	33.4
% of Livestock Value	0.0	0.1	1.2	5.3	12.5	9.4	5.3	15.4	11.3	60.5
% of Non-Slaveholding Farmers	16.7	4.3	17.0	15.6	9.0	2.5	0.9	0.5	0.1	66.6
% of Livestock Value	0.0	0.4	5.4	10.1	11.1	5.6	2.9	2.4	1.6	39.5

1860

$ Value of Livestock	0	1-99	100-249	250-499	500-999	1,000-1,499	1,500-1,999	2,000-4,999	5,000+	Totals
% of Farm Population	20.0	1.6	10.6	18.9	20.9	10.0	5.7	9.7	2.6	100.0
% of Livestock Value	0.0	0.1	1.8	6.7	14.7	11.8	9.7	28.5	26.7	100.0
% of Slaveholding Farmers	1.8	0.1	0.9	4.1	8.0	5.3	3.2	6.6	2.1	32.1
% of Livestock Value	0.0	0.0	0.1	1.5	5.8	6.4	5.4	19.6	21.3	60.1
% of Non-Slaveholding Farmers	18.2	1.5	9.7	14.8	12.9	4.7	2.5	3.1	0.5	67.9
% of Livestock Value	0.0	0.1	1.7	5.2	8.9	5.4	4.3	8.9	5.4	39.9

production of wheat, oats, rye, and barley combined.[6] Thus, distributions of the corn crop may well be taken as indicators of the degree of equality or inequality in general farm production during the 1850's.

The degree of concentration in corn production was high in both 1850 and 1860; in fact the corn crop was more highly concentrated than either improved acreage or livestock value among our sample agricultural populations (see table 25). The relative positions of small, medium, and large producers of corn remained fairly stable during the 1850's (table 29), although those who grew 2,000 or more bushels did increase their share of the corn crop more rapidly (from 23.9 to 28.9 percent of the total) than they increased as a proportion of the agricultural population. As was true of improved acreage, cash value, and livestock value, the one-third of the farm population who held slaves accounted for approximately two-thirds of all corn production. Actually the slaveholding farmers' share of the corn crop increased more rapidly than their share of any other item of agricultural property and production during the 1850's.

Cotton Production, 1850-1860

The importance of cotton as an indicator of economic status among farmers obviously does not require argument. In antebellum Texas, cotton was the heart of the agricultural market economy. And in general it was the best measure of a farmer's income. Historians have long recognized the significance of cotton production for the questions of wealthholding, but as Morton Rothstein pointed out in 1970, we do not know precisely the relative positions of small, medium, and large cotton planters and the extent to which each shared in production for the market economy.[7]

[6]The 1850 and 1860 censuses recorded crop production during the years ending June 1, 1850, and June 1, 1860. Therefore, the corn and cotton figures recorded in these censuses refer to the 1849 and 1859 crops.

[7]Morton Rothstein, "The Cotton Frontier of the Antebellum United States: A Methodological Battleground," *Agricultural History* 44 (January, 1970), 160.

TABLE 29

DISTRIBUTION OF CORN PRODUCTION, 1850 AND 1860

1850

Bushels of Corn	0	1-99	100-249	250-499	500-999	1,000-1,499	1,500-1,999	2,000-4,999	5,000+	Totals
% of Farm Population	30.0	6.7	24.3	18.3	12.6	4.2	1.2	2.3	0.4	100.0
% of Corn Crop	0.0	1.1	11.6	18.8	24.5	14.0	6.0	17.2	6.7	99.9
% of Slaveholding Farmers	5.7	1.4	5.3	6.6	7.5	3.4	1.1	2.1	0.3	33.4
% of Corn Crop	0.0	0.2	2.6	7.1	14.9	11.4	5.9	16.3	6.2	64.6
% of Non-Slaveholding Farmers	24.3	5.3	19.0	11.7	5.1	0.8	0.1	0.2	0.1	66.6
% of Corn Crop	0.0	0.9	9.0	11.7	9.6	2.6	0.1	0.9	0.5	35.4

1860

% of Farm Population	30.0	9.0	24.1	17.2	10.9	3.8	2.1	2.4	0.5	100.0
% of Corn Crop	0.0	1.3	10.8	16.6	20.1	12.5	9.8	18.2	10.7	100.0
% of Slaveholding Farmers	4.1	1.3	5.1	6.3	7.2	3.3	2.0	2.3	0.5	32.1
% of Corn Crop	0.0	0.2	2.4	6.5	13.7	10.9	9.7	17.8	10.7	71.9
% of Non-Slaveholding Farmers	25.9	7.7	19.0	10.9	3.6	0.5	0.1	0.1	0.0	67.8
% of Corn Crop	0.0	1.1	8.4	10.1	6.4	1.6	0.1	0.4	0.0	28.1

Cotton production was far more concentrated in the hands of a small group of farmers during the 1850's than was improved acreage, cash value of farms, livestock value, or the corn crop. The Gini index of .906 in 1850 (table 25) was extremely high. In 1860 the degree of concentration remained very high (Gini of .880), but it should be noted that the level of concentration in cotton, unlike that for the other items of agricultural property and production, decreased slightly from 1850 to 1860. A slight decline of this sort should be expected, however, in measurements of inequality in the production of a rapidly expanding market crop. A look at the relative positions of small, medium, and large producers of cotton will reveal that the slight decrease in concentration took place under circumstances that were actually shifting even more in favor of the large planter class.

Table 30 demonstrates a sharp decrease in the percentage of farmers who grew no cotton, but it also indicates a decline in the relative positions of small (1 to 9 bales) and medium (10 to 49 bales) cotton producers. Both groups increased as a percentage of the total population, but at the same time both saw their share of the cotton crop decline markedly. Planters who grew 50 or more bales increased from 1.2 to 4.3 percent of the farming population, and their part of the cotton crop jumped from 32.1 to 60.9 percent. The degree of concentration declined slightly due to the smaller percentage of non-cotton growers and the fact that large planters increased more rapidly as a percentage of the total than did their share of the whole crop. Nevertheless, the group of small farmers producing fewer than 10 bales controlled only 10.5 percent of the crop in 1860, less than half as much as the 23.7 percent controlled by this group in 1850. Meanwhile fewer than 5 percent of the large planters produced 60.9 percent of all cotton.

As might be expected, slaveholding farmers enjoyed a wide margin of superiority over non-slaveholders in the production of cotton, far wider than in livestock or corn, for example. The obvious importance of slave labor in cash-crop cultivation is attested to by the fact that the one-third of the agricultural population who held bondsmen produced approximately

TABLE 30

DISTRIBUTION OF COTTON PRODUCTION, 1850 AND 1860

1850

Bales of Cotton	0	1-4	5-9	10-19	20-49	50-99	100-149	150-199	200+	Totals
% of Farm Population	75.6	12.4	5.4	2.6	2.8	0.9	0.1	0.1	0.1	100.0
% of Cotton Crop	0.0	10.5	13.2	12.8	31.4	21.4	5.7	1.6	3.4	100.0
% of Slaveholding Farmers	18.6	4.8	3.7	2.3	2.8	0.9	0.1	0.1	0.1	33.4
% of Cotton Crop	0.0	4.7	9.1	11.5	31.4	21.4	5.7	1.6	3.4	88.8
% of Non-Slaveholding Farmers	57.0	7.6	1.7	0.3	0.0	0.0	0.0	0.0	0.0	66.6
% of Cotton Crop	0.0	5.8	4.1	1.3	0.0	0.0	0.0	0.0	0.0	11.2

1860

Bales of Cotton	0	1-4	5-9	10-19	20-49	50-99	100-149	150-199	200+	Totals
% of Farm Population	60.9	14.9	8.4	6.4	5.1	2.6	0.8	0.4	0.5	100.0
% of Cotton Crop	0.0	4.0	6.5	10.1	18.5	21.3	11.7	7.1	20.8	100.0
% of Slaveholding Farmers	11.7	2.8	3.6	4.9	4.9	2.6	0.8	0.4	0.5	32.2
% of Cotton Crop	0.0	0.9	2.9	7.9	18.0	21.3	11.7	7.1	20.8	90.6
% of Non-Slaveholding Farmers	49.2	12.1	4.8	1.5	0.2	0.0	0.0	0.0	0.0	67.8
% of Cotton Crop	0.0	3.1	3.6	2.2	0.5	0.0	0.0	0.0	0.0	9.4

90 percent of all cotton in both 1850 and 1860. There were no producers of 50 or more bales in either census year who held no slaves. On the other hand, the great majority who grew no cotton were non-slaveholders.

In summary, cotton, the primary cash crop of antebellum Texas' agricultural economy, was very highly concentrated in the hands of a small group of large planters, all of whom were slaveholders in our sample. Small farmers, a majority of whom were non-slaveholders, had a declining share of the cotton crop and participated in a much less meaningful way in the market economy in 1860 than in 1850.

Regions of Antebellum Texas, 1850-1860

Region I, the east Texas timberland area, was even more agricultural than the state as a whole in 1850 and 1860. Individuals engaged in farming constituted 87.6 percent of the regional sample population in 1850 and 81.8 percent in 1860 compared with 77.4 percent and 74.4 percent statewide in those years. Table 24 demonstrates that slaveholders were a little more than one-third of the farming population, a slightly greater percentage than they represented in the whole state's agricultural population, and that few slaveholders owned no acreage. The percentage of landless farmers in region I, both slaveholding and non-slaveholding, declined from 1850 to 1860, a development that did not take place statewide. Perhaps some landless farmers acquired land of their own during the 1850's, or perhaps they simply left the region in search of opportunities elsewhere or went into other occupations. Farmers did decline as a percentage of the total population in region I from 1850 to 1860 (see table 3). Nevertheless it is interesting that an apparent expansion of landholding, however slight it may have been, occurred in an older, more highly settled area rather than in a frontier region where it might have been expected.

The Gini indices presented in table 25 indicate that in general improved acreage, farm value, livestock value, corn, and cotton were less concentrated in region I than in the state as a whole. And unlike the situation statewide, all indices except the measurement for livestock value decreased during the 1850's. All these variations and changes are slight, certainly not great enough to indicate that region I differed much from the state as a whole in having moderately high to high levels of inequality in agricultural property and production. Nevertheless, there appears to have been a slightly greater degree of equality among the farming population of east Texas than among farmers statewide.

It is almost impossible to generalize concerning the relative positions of small, medium, and larger farmers in region I compared with the same groups in the state as a whole. There are simply too many variations in the sizes of comparable groups and their shares of the property or crop involved from one category of agricultural property and production to another in 1850 and 1860. In the case of region I, however, it is possible to say that middle groups, those holding 50 to 299 improved acres or producing 100 to 1,999 bushels of corn, for example, generally constituted a larger proportion of the farming population and held a larger share of farm property and production than did the comparable group statewide in both 1850 and 1860.[8]

Slaveholders constituted a larger group in the farm population of region I in both 1850 and 1860 than they did among farmers in the state as a whole (see table 24). And in constrast to the trend statewide, they increased, however slightly, as a group during the decade. Although these slaveowners held a disproportionately large share of improved acreage, farm value, livestock value, corn, and cotton very comparable to the holdings of slaveowning farmers in the state as a whole, they, as a slightly larger group, did not enjoy quite the advantage in controlling agricultural property and production enjoyed by slaveholders statewide.

The Gulf coastal region of antebellum Texas (region II) had a relatively small proportion of its population, 50 percent in 1850 and 33.3 percent in 1860, directly engaged in agriculture. Of course, the presence

[8]Tables showing the distributions of agricultural property and production for all four regions for 1850 and 1860 among the entire farming population, slaveholders, and nonslaveholders are in appendix 3.

of Galveston and Houston explains this situation. Approximately 50 percent of the farmers were slaveholders (see table 24), indicating that the ownership of bondsmen was much more important in this area of large plantations than it was statewide. Between 1850 and 1860, landless farmers declined from 19.4 to 11.4 percent of the farm population, but this development may be explained primarily in terms of the noticeable decrease in the percentage of farmers in the total population during that period. As material presented below will demonstrate, Gulf coastal Texas was not a likely region for the advancement of small farmers.

With the single exception of cotton in 1860, every category of agricultural property and production was more highly concentrated in region II than statewide (see table 25). But in this case not even the high indices of concentration fully reveal the extent of economic domination by the big planters. Compared with the situation in the state as a whole in 1850 and 1860, large farmers were a far greater percentage of the agricultural population in coastal Texas, and this group held a much greater proportion of total agricultural property and production. In the case of cotton, for example, producers of 50 or more bales constituted 4.3 percent of the farmers statewide compared with 14.1 percent in region II, and those large farmers' shares of the cotton crop were 60.8 and 85.7 percent respectively. At the same time, of course, the relative position of farmers with small and medium holdings in region II was notably inferior to that of these groups statewide.

In 1850, 46.2 percent of region II's farmers were slaveholders, whereas only 33.4 percent of the state's agricultural population owned bondsmen (see table 24). By 1860, in contrast to the slight decline in this group statewide, slaveholding farmers in region II increased to a majority, 55.8 percent, of the agricultural population. In every category of farm property and production except livestock value, slaveowners controlled approximately 90 percent of the total; in cotton production they had a virtual monopoly. Clearly, agriculture in the coastal region was dominated by slaveholding planters in a manner that did not exist statewide in either 1850 or 1860.

The population of region III, the more "frontier" north-central Texas area, was more than 90 percent agricultural in 1850, and ten years later this region still had a relatively high proportion of its people engaged in farming. Slaveholders constituted a noticeably smaller part of the farm population in region III than they did statewide in 1850 and 1860. Unlike the situation across antebellum Texas, however, the percentage of slave-owning farmers increased in the north-central region during the 1850's (see table 24). Curiously, there was an increase in the landless farmer class from 13.5 percent of the total in 1850 to 25.8 percent in 1860. At first glance, it seems strange that landless farmers increased in a more western, "frontier" region. But perhaps the explanation lies in the very rapid growth of this area during the decade. With a population expanding more rapidly than in any other region, region III in 1860 may simply have had more recent arrivals who had not yet acquired their own land.

In 1850 Gini indices of concentration for agricultural property and production in region III were in general slightly lower than those indices statewide (see table 25). This is especially noticeable in the case of improved acreage, where the Gini for region III (.454) indicates a medium level of concentration compared with the higher degree in the state as a whole (.597). Cotton was an exception to the "rule" of less concentration in region III in 1850, but there were so few cotton farmers in this newly settled area that the extremely high Gini index is not as reliable an indicator of economic inequality as the other categories, such as improved acreage. The Gini indices for 1860 demonstrate that the degree of concentration in region III advanced during the last antebellum decade to a level closely comparable to that for the state as a whole.

Farmers who held large amounts of agricultural property and produced the largest crops of corn and cotton constituted a somewhat smaller group in region III than they did statewide in 1850. For example, only 0.1 percent of region III's farmers owned 300 or more improved acres in 1850 compared with 1 percent of all farmers in Texas. By 1860, however, the proportions of large holders statewide and in region III in all categories were more nearly equal, and a comparison of the distributions of agricultural property and production among small and medium holders in the state and the region reveals no important general variations. Slaveholders constituted a significantly smaller group of the farming population in region III than they did statewide in both 1850 and 1860. But they increased during the decade, and their already disproportionately large share of agricultural property and production increased even more rapidly. In short, the north-central Texas area as it grew and matured during the 1850's may not have expanded in quite the same way as other regions; nevertheless, the effect was an increase in the degree of economic inequality among the farming population by 1860.

Region IV, south-central Texas, had a lower percentage of farmers in its population than did the state as a whole in 1850 and 1860. This may be explained largely in terms of the location of San Antonio and the rapidly growing town of Austin in the region. But the percentage of farmers in the population of region IV, unlike that for the entire state or any other region, increased between 1850 and 1860 (see table 1). There does not appear to be any special explanation for this increase. Region IV with its large German population had sizable, growing towns, but its farming population simply expanded more rapidly than its non-farming population. Moreover, as the farming population of the south-central Texas area increased, the percentage of landless farmers did not rise appreciably. Indeed, region IV had a slightly smaller proportion of farmers without land than did the state as a whole in both 1850 and 1860.

Although the distribution of its population according to occupational and slaveholding status may have varied somewhat from that of the state as a whole, region IV was the area most like antebellum Texas in general. As chapter 2 pointed out, this region had areas of large plantations, small farms, frontier settlement, and yet there were also several sizable towns. Thus, in most areas of comparison with circumstances statewide, measures of inequality in the ownership of agricultural property and production are very similar. Table 25 demonstrates that state and region IV Gini indices of concentration were virtually identical in 1850, and that by 1860, with the exception of the index for cotton, they were only slightly higher in region IV than statewide. The relative positions of small, medium, and large farmers were so similar from one category to another that no significant pattern of variation between the state and the region emerges. There was a tendency in region IV toward greater percentages of large farmers holding larger proportions of property and crops by 1860, but it was far from pronounced. Slaveholding farmers constituted almost exactly the same percentage of region IV's agricultural population as they did statewide, and their shares of improved acreage, farm value, and other measures were equally large and disproportionate to their numbers.

After examination of the agricultural population of the state as a whole in 1850 and 1860 and comparison of the various regions with the whole in both years, only one question remains — how did the four regions compare with each other? Were there areas that clearly had greater or lesser degrees of inequality than others in the distribution of agricultural property and production during the last antebellum decade?

In general, region II, the Gulf coastal area stretching from the Sabine River to Calhoun and Victoria counties, was more dominated by large slaveholding planters than any other region. With the single exception of the measurement for livestock in 1860, Gini indices for improved acreage, farm value, and the like in region II were greater than .667 and thus may be classified as "high." In most cases these indices were higher in 1850 in region II than in the other regions. Ten years later improved acreage and farm value were still more highly concentrated in region II, and in other categories the region was second in the degree of concentration (see table 25). The largest farmers, those holding 300 or more acres of improved land or producing 50 or more bales of cotton, for example, constituted virtually twice as large a percentage of the agricultural population in region II as they did in any other area. Slaveholding farmers were also a significantly greater proportion of the whole there, and they owned nearly 90 percent of all property and products except livestock and very close to 100 percent of cotton production. Actually, by 1860 slaveholders were such a large group in region II that they, as individuals, held on the average smaller shares (not absolute values) of agricultural property and production than did slaveholders in other regions. However, as a group, slaveholding farmers were clearly more dominant in the Gulf coastal area than anywhere else in the state.

It is extremely difficult to say that any region had a noticeably lower degree of economic inequality than the others among its farm population. Region III, north-central Texas, had somewhat lower Gini indices in 1850, slaveholders were a smaller group there, and there were fewer large farmers. But by 1860, region I, which had more big holders and a higher percentage of slaveholders than did region III, had lower indices of concentration in every category than did any other region. In region IV, which was almost a composite of the state as a whole, the various measurements of inequality generally fell somewhere between the highest and lowest measures for the other three regions. Thus, there were some variations from one area to another in levels of concentration, relative positions of small, medium, and large farmers, and proportions of slaveholders in the population. Nevertheless the most striking fact demonstrated is the consistently high degree of inequality overall in the farming population of all regions.

Summary

In summary, then, the agricultural population of antebellum Texas, which accounted for three-quarters of all the state's families, was characterized by moderately high to high levels of concentration in the distribution of key farm properties and products in 1850 and 1860. There was very little change in the degree of concentration during the last antebellum decade. In general, the slight shifts that occurred followed an upward trend, especially in the rapidly developing region of north-central Texas. Cotton, the key crop in the market economy, was far more highly concentrated than other properties and products.

A small group of large farmers, generally less than 5 percent of the total, consistently held a disproportionately large share of improved acreage, farm value, livestock value, corn, and cotton. From 1850 to 1860 the percentage of farmers in this group of large holders increased a little more rapidly than their share of farm properties and products, so their increase did not cause a significant jump in the Gini indices of concentration. Nevertheless, as a group, the small minority of large farmers, still less than 5 percent of the total, were in a more commanding position in 1860 than they had been at the beginning of the decade. Small farmers generally decreased as a percentage of the total population, but their share of improved acreage, farm value, and other categories declined even more rapidly. Still a sizable group, small farmers were in a weaker position relative to other groups in 1860 than in 1850. The group of farmers with medium holdings generally increased or remained stable depending on the category of property and production under consideration. At the same time, their share of property and crops frequently declined to some degree from 1850 to 1860. Thus, large farmers were the only group in the farm population that consistently increased in size and share of agricultural property and production during the 1850's.

Slaveholding farmers, constituting approximately one-third of the agricultural population statewide, enjoyed control of between 60 and 70 percent of improved acreage, farm value, livestock value, and corn production. In the case of cotton, slaveowners produced approximately 90 percent of the crop in both census years. There were some noticeable variations in the percentages of slaveholders in the farming population from region to region. Region II, the Gulf coastal area, had by far the greatest proportion of slaveholders, whereas region III, north-central Texas, had a far smaller percentage than any other area. Wherever they were, however, slaveholders held a disproportionately large share of farm property and production and represented a strong element of inequality in the agricultural population. Finally, when we consider the evidence presented by Gini indices of concentration, a comparison of the relative positions of small, medium, and large farmers, and a description of the commanding position of the slaveholding minority, it seems very clear that there was a significantly high degree of economic inequality among the agricultural population of antebellum Texas.

The economic class structure revealed in this chapter supports the contention of Frank L. Owsley and his disciples that there was a large and growing middle class in the antebellum South. More thorough analysis, however, indicates that the Owsley school should have asked more questions of their data. There may have been a sizable and increasing yeoman-farmer class in antebellum Texas, but what share of the state's agricultural property and production did this group control? The answer, as shown here, places Texas much closer to the planter-dominance thesis of Phillips and Gray than to the yeoman-farmer view held by Owsley.

Chapter 6.

Wealthholding in Texas Towns, 1850-1860

ALTHOUGH farmers made up the bulk of antebellum Texas' population, the state did contain four sizable towns in the 1850's — Galveston and Houston in the coastal plain region and San Antonio and Austin on the rolling hills and prairies of the south-central counties. These towns in no way qualified as cities by northeastern United States standards, but they were Texas' main centers of transportation, communication, commerce, and government. Thus, they qualify as urban areas in a predominantly rural state.[1]

Of the four, only San Antonio predated the 1830's, the others having been founded during the troubled decade that culminated in the Texas Revolution of 1836. San Antonio was founded in 1718 as a Spanish military outpost. After winning undying fame in Texas history as the site of the battle of the Alamo in 1836, San Antonio was made the county seat of Bexar County in 1837. With an overwhelmingly Mexican population in the pre-Revolution era, the town began attracting large numbers of Anglo-Americans and foreigners in the 1830's and 1840's, and by 1850 San Antonio contained about 3,500 inhabitants. Rapid growth in the 1850's more than doubled the population to roughly 8,200 in 1860, making San Antonio the largest town in Texas. Oldest, largest, and most heavily Mexican, San Antonio was unique among the large towns of antebellum Texas.

The other three sizable towns — Galveston, Houston, and Austin — were primarily Anglo-American in origin and population rather than

[1]The importance of these four towns is recognized in Kenneth W. Wheeler, *To Wear a City's Crown: The Beginnings of Urban Growth in Texas, 1836-1865*.

Spanish or Mexican. Galveston, the largest town in the state in 1850 (with a population of 4,117) and second largest in 1860 (population of 7,307), predated Houston and Austin by several years. Established as a small Mexican military post in 1830 or 1831, the town did not experience rapid growth until after the Texas Revolution in the mid-1830's. It was made a port of entry for the Republic of Texas in 1837 and named county seat of Galveston County in 1839. With an excellent harbor and with a newspaper, chamber of commerce, and school founded in the mid-1840's, Galveston became the major port and city of the republic.

Houston, fifty miles northwest of Galveston, began in 1836 when two New York-born brothers organized the town from the ground up. John and Augustus Allen purchased the land, laid out town lots, and advertised their creation in the newborn republic until a steady stream of immigrants began moving into their new town. Incorporated in 1837, Houston was county seat of Harris County and also briefly served as the capital of the republic until the rough, frontier village of Austin snatched away the seat of government in 1839.

Houston prospered and grew in the 1830's and 1840's, serving the republic and state as a major commercial center and as an important cotton port. With a population of 2,400 by 1850, the town doubled in size to over 4,800 by the eve of the Civil War.

The frontier settlement of Austin, youngest and smallest of the four major towns, was planned from the beginning as the capital of the Republic of Texas. Construction began on public buildings in May, 1839, and by October government officials and a newspaper were operating despite the ever-present danger of Mexican and Indian attacks. These threatened and real invasions prevented any solid growth for several years, and by 1850 Austin's population was still a tiny 629. The 1850's brought more safety and stability, however, and the town enjoyed a small boom, resulting in a fivefold increase in population to about 3,500 by 1860.[2]

[2]For background information on Texas towns, see Walter Prescott Webb et al., eds., *The Handbook of Texas; The Texas Almanac and State Industrial Guide*, published annually; and especially Wheeler, *To Wear a City's Crown*.

Characteristics of Urban Texans

In all the larger towns of Texas the proportion of the population that was foreign-born exceeded that for the state as a whole (for statewide figures, see table 2). Indeed, in San Antonio, Galveston, and Houston the foreign element ranged between one-third and one-half of the town populations in both 1850 and 1860. In frontier Austin the percentage was in the mid-teens in both years (see table 31).[3]

San Antonio's foreign-born were primarily Mexicans and Germans in both 1850 and 1860, but roughly one-fourth of the foreigners were from Ireland, France, England, and various other countries. Germans constituted about two-thirds of Galveston's foreign population in the 1850's with other European-born immigrants making up most of the remainder. Houston had fewer foreigners than either San Antonio or Galveston, but the origins of its foreign-born element followed the same pattern as in Galveston in both 1850 and 1860 — roughly two-thirds were Germans and most of the rest were from other European countries. Austin, younger and more isolated from the major seaports and Mexican communities than the other towns, had far fewer foreigners in both absolute numbers and in proportions — only 15.1 percent in 1850 and 16.8 percent in 1860. Nevertheless, the capital was similar to Galveston and Houston in the pattern of foreign birthplaces — about two-thirds German and the remainder mostly European.

The differences between the urban and statewide populations did not stop there, for townspeople also diverged from the general state pattern in the occupations pursued by heads of families (see table 32).[4]

[3]The figures on foreign population in the text and in table 31 were taken from the United States Censuses of 1850 and 1860 and appeared originally in Ralph A. Wooster, "Foreigners in the Principal Towns of Ante-Bellum Texas," *Southwestern Historical Quarterly* 66 (October, 1962), 208-209. If only heads of families are counted (rather than total population as in Wooster's article), the foreign element in the towns is even larger — 56.5 percent of the total in 1850 and 60.6 percent in 1860. These figures, which will be used later in this chapter, are from our samples.

[4]All tables and statistics, unless otherwise cited, are taken from our samples of the 1850 and 1860 manuscript censuses.

TABLE 31

FOREIGNERS IN LARGE TEXAS TOWNS, 1850 AND 1860

	San Antonio	Galveston	Houston	Austin
1850				
Germans	412	1,088	425	60
Mexicans	570	8	6	2
Irish	118	108	49	6
English	34	157	50	8
French	78	110	45	4
Others	52	122	23	15
Percent of Foreigners	39.0	48.0	32.0	15.1
1860				
Germans	1,477	1,613	816	255
Mexicans	1,220	10	17	24
Irish	310	344	241	30
English	68	300	114	32
French	232	182	62	8
Others	294	249	100	75
Percent of Foreigners	47.1	44.0	35.7	16.8

TABLE 32

OCCUPATIONS IN ANTEBELLUM TEXAS, 1850 AND 1860

(In Percentages)

	1850		1860	
	Whole State	Urban Texas	Whole State	Urban Texas
Farmers	71.3	2.5	69.7	5.5
Commerce	3.8	15.6	4.3	17.5
Professional	5.4	11.1	5.1	8.8
Public Officials	0.7	2.2	0.8	2.2
Manufacturers	1.1	0.7	1.1	0.7
Skilled Tradesmen	10.8	37.0	9.2	32.1
Unskilled Services	5.9	28.1	9.2	29.2
Miscellaneous	1.0	2.8	0.6	4.0
Totals	100.0	100.0	100.0	100.0

While roughly three-fourths of Texas family heads were farmers (including stock raisers and overseers), less than 3 percent of the urban families were engaged in agriculture in 1850 and less than 6 percent in 1860. In addition, although skilled artisans (carpenters, gunsmiths, blacksmiths, printers, and tailors) and unskilled workers (wagoners, manual laborers) made up only about one-sixth of the state's total household heads in both census years (16.7 percent in 1850 and 18.4 percent in 1860), this occupation group accounted for nearly four-sixths of the urban population (65.1 percent in 1850 and 61.3 percent in 1860). After skilled and unskilled workers, the largest occupation group in the large towns was the commercial class (merchants, salesmen, real estate agents, grocers, etc.). This group, dominated financially and numerically by the merchants, was proportionately four times larger in the towns than in the whole state (15.6 percent in 1850 and 17.5 percent in 1860 in the towns as opposed to 3.8 percent in 1850 and 4.3 percent in 1860 statewide). As expected, the professional class (lawyers, physicians, ministers, teachers) was proportionately twice as large in the towns as in the whole state. Interestingly, manufacturers (furniture makers, wagon and carriage makers, brick makers) were a numerically insignificant group in the towns as well as the state as a whole in both census years, emphasizing once again that the antebellum Texas economy was overwhelmingly rural and agricultural. In short, the urban Texas population, while it contained very few farmers, included (proportionately) four times as many skilled and unskilled laborers, four times as many merchants, and twice as many professionals as the statewide population.

As for differences in property holdings, fewer town families owned slaves than in the state as a whole — 30.1 percent in 1850 and 27.3 percent in 1860 statewide (see table 9) and only 15.9 percent in 1850 and 11.7 percent in 1860 in the towns (see table 34). In addition, urban slaveholding families generally owned fewer slaves than in the state as a unit; the statewide average was 7.2 slaves per head of household in 1850 and 9.4 in 1860, whereas in the towns the means dropped to 4.0 in 1850 and 5.6 in 1860. A different pattern emerges in real and personal property, however. Statewide, Texas heads of households averaged $1,461 worth of real property in 1850 and $2,699 in 1860; in the towns the means were somewhat higher — $1,857 in 1850 and $4,773 in 1860. Wealth, a combination of real and personal property, averaged $6,393 per family statewide in 1860 and $7,814 per family in the towns.

Thus, compared with the typical Texas family head, the urban dweller was less likely to be a native American, less likely to be a farmer, less likely to own slaves, less likely to be a large slaveowner if he did own bondsmen, but more likely to own more real or personal property.[5]

Wealthholding

Although property was very unequally distributed in the state as a whole, as we have demonstrated in chapter 3, the inequality is even more striking in Texas towns. The Gini index for real property, high (.780) for Texas as a whole in 1850, was even higher (.868) in towns; that is, real property was less equally distributed in urban areas than in the state as a unit.

Indeed, over half the town families owned no real property at all. Table 33 shows that the richest 4.7 percent of the urban heads of families (those owning $10,000 or more of real property) controlled 62 percent of all town-owned real estate in 1850. By contrast, the poorest 61.5 percent of urban families (those controlling less than $250 of such property) owned less than 1 percent of the real property.

The same pattern emerges in slaveholdings. The statewide Gini index for slave property in 1850 was .855, but the urban index was even higher at .903. Among town families 84.1 percent owned no slaves at all,

[5]All these mean figures, for the state and for the towns, were accompanied by high standard deviations. High standard deviations, as we have here, mean that the property holdings varied widely above and below the average. The higher means on real and personal property for town families is explained mainly by the presence of a relatively few extremely wealthy families in the towns whose property holdings raised the average for all urban heads of households. High standard deviations support this conclusion. The standard deviations on the urban measurements of real and personal estate were about three times higher than the averages and were greater than the standard deviations for the state as a whole, which ranged between two and three times the statewide means.

TABLE 33

DISTRIBUTION OF REAL PROPERTY IN LARGE TEXAS TOWNS, 1850 AND 1860

1850

Size of Holding	$0	$1–249	$250–499	$500–999	$1,000–4,999	$5,000–9,999	$10,000–19,999	$20,000–49,999	$50,000 and up	Totals
Percent of Property Holders	51.5	10.0	5.3	7.5	15.6	5.3	2.5	1.4	0.8	100.0
Percent of Real Property	0.0	0.8	0.9	2.5	16.1	17.7	17.2	20.8	24.0	100.0

1860

Size of Holding	$0	$1–249	$250–499	$500–999	$1,000–4,999	$5,000–9,999	$10,000–19,999	$20,000–49,999	$50,000 and up	Totals
Percent of Property Holders	56.2	1.8	2.2	6.2	16.8	4.7	3.7	4.7	3.6	100.0
Percent of Real Property	0.0	0.1	0.2	0.8	7.8	6.5	9.6	28.7	46.4	100.0

whereas the largest 1.4 percent (those owning ten or more bondsmen) controlled 29.2 percent of all urban slaves (see table 34).

In summary, then, both real and slave property were highly concentrated in a few hands in Texas towns in 1850, even more highly concentrated than in the state as a whole.

The situation did not change much by 1860. The statewide Gini index for real property remained stable, going from .780 in 1850 to .786 in 1860. The urban index also remained virtually level, moving only from .868 in 1850 to .863 in 1860. In both years the town index was significantly higher than the statewide index. One difference did appear: by 1860 there were more very wealthy holders and slightly fewer who owned little or nothing. That is, those town dwellers who owned $10,000 or more of real estate jumped from 4.7 percent of the urban total in 1850 to 12 percent in 1860. As table 33 demonstrates, those 12 percent controlled 84.7 percent of all town-owned real property. At the lower end of the scale, the poorest 58 percent (those who held less than $250) owned only one-tenth of 1 percent of the real estate.

TABLE 34

DISTRIBUTION OF SLAVE PROPERTY IN LARGE TEXAS TOWNS, 1850 AND 1860

1850

Number of Slaves	0	1-4	5-9	10-19	20-29	30-39	40-49	50-99	100 and up	Totals
Percent of Slave-holders	84.1	10.6	3.9	1.4	0.0	0.0	0.0	0.0	0.0	100.0
Percent of Slaves	0.0	31.4	39.4	29.2	0.0	0.0	0.0	0.0	0.0	100.0

1860

Number of Slaves	0	1-4	5-9	10-19	20-29	30-39	40-49	50-99	100 and up	Totals
Percent of Slave-holders	88.3	6.2	3.7	1.8	0.0	0.0	0.0	0.0	0.0	100.0
Percent of Slaves	0.0	22.5	39.3	38.2	0.0	0.0	0.0	0.0	0.0	100.0

Personal property, not recorded in the 1850 census but tabulated in 1860, followed the same general pattern as real estate. The Gini index of .894 is clearly higher than the statewide index of .756 for personal property and reflects the fact that the wealthiest 6.9 percent of town families (those owning $10,000 or more of personal property) controlled 76.9 percent of the personal estate (see table 35). On the poorer end, the 64.2

TABLE 35

DISTRIBUTION OF PERSONAL PROPERTY IN LARGE TEXAS TOWNS, 1860

Size of Holding	$0	$1-249	$250-499	$500-999	$1,000-4,999	$5,000-9,999	$10,000-19,999	$20,000-49,999	$50,000 and up	Totals
Percent of Property Holders	59.8	4.4	4.7	3.7	13.9	6.6	2.5	2.6	1.8	100.0
Percent of Personal Property	0.0	0.2	0.5	0.7	8.8	12.9	11.3	23.0	42.6	100.0

percent of the people who owned less than $250 worth of personal property controlled only two-tenths of 1 percent of town-owned personal estate.

The measurements on wealth, a combination of real and personal property in 1860, must necessarily closely follow the pattern established for those two forms of property, and indeed they do. With a Gini index of .849, again higher than the statewide index of .742 for wealth, table 36 shows the richest 9.9 percent of urban families (those with $20,000 or more in wealth) owning 78.5 percent of the wealth, whereas the poorest 49.6 percent (those with less than $500) had only three-tenths of 1 percent of the town-owned wealth.

Finally, the highest concentration in this entire study was in town-owned slaves in 1860. The Gini index for urban slave property in 1850 was a stunning .903, but it was even higher in 1860 at .926. Compare this with the statewide index of .876 for 1860 slave property, and it is obvious that urban slaves, though fewer in number than rural bondsmen, were even more highly concentrated in a few hands. Table 34 demonstrates that nearly 90 percent of town families owned no slaves at all, whereas the wealthiest 1.8 percent (those with ten or more bondsmen) controlled 38.2 percent of all slaves.[6] Not one of the urban family heads in our sample, however, owned as many as twenty bondsmen, either in 1850 or 1860.

To recapitulate, the high indices of concentration for urban-owned property in 1850 remained high or were somewhat higher by 1860. Real property was about as unequally distributed in 1850 as in 1860, but slaveholdings were slightly more concentrated in a few hands in the latter year. Personal property and wealth (as a combination of real and personal estate) were not tabulated in the 1850 census, but they would doubtless

[6]In a sense, the Gini index can be misleading. When over 90 percent of the family heads considered do not own a certain type of property (e.g., urban slaves), such property is obviously highly concentrated in the hands of a small minority, but at the same time the huge majority of the families are "equal" in that they own no slaves. Thus, it is possible to have a situation of high concentration and relative equality coexisting with each other. As we have indicated earlier, the Gini index should always be considered in conjunction with the distribution upon which it is based for a full understanding of the property-holding situation.

TABLE 36

DISTRIBUTION OF WEALTH IN LARGE TEXAS TOWNS, 1860

Size of Holding	$0	$1-249	$250-499	$500-999	$1,000-4,999	$5,000-9,999	$10,000-19,999	$20,000-49,999	$50,000 and up	Totals
Percent of Wealth Holders	42.7	2.2	4.7	7.7	20.8	6.9	5.1	4.4	5.5	100.0
Percent of Wealth	0.0	0.1	0.2	0.6	5.9	5.9	8.9	18.2	60.3	100.0

show a similar pattern. In all cases, property owned by town dwellers was more highly concentrated among the wealthiest families than was property in Texas as a whole.

Slaveholding

Although slaveholders were proportionately fewer and generally smaller in the towns than they were statewide, nevertheless town-dwelling slaveowners generally controlled a larger share of non-slave property each than did their counterparts in the whole state. As mentioned in chapter 3, 30.1 percent of all families in the state in 1850 owned slaves, and these households controlled 71.8 percent of all real property, a significant edge for the slaveholding class. This feature of Texas wealth distribution is even more pronounced in the towns, however, where only 15.9 percent of the urban families were slaveowners and yet they held 67.6 percent of the real property (see table 37). By 1860 slaveholding households in all of Texas had declined slightly to 27.3 percent of all families, but their share of real property had edged upward to 74.7 percent. This slightly greater share for slaveowners statewide still did not approach the share held by urban slaveholders, however. In the towns only 11.7 percent of all families owned bondsmen in 1860, but their share of real property was 57.4 percent, proportionately higher than 1850 and proportionately higher than the statewide figure.

TABLE 37

DISTRIBUTION OF REAL PROPERTY AMONG SLAVEHOLDERS AND NON-SLAVEHOLDERS IN LARGE TEXAS TOWNS, 1850 AND 1860

1850

Size of Holding	$0	$1-249	$250-499	$500-999	$1,000-4,999	$5,000-9,999	$10,000-19,999	$20,000-49,999	$50,000 and up	Totals
Percent of Population Who Were Slaveholders	3.0	0.0	0.0	0.3	4.7	3.9	2.0	1.4	0.6	15.9
Percent of Property Owned by Slaveholders	0.0	0.0	0.0	0.1	4.9	13.1	12.2	20.8	16.5	67.6
Percent of Population Who Were Non-Slaveholders	48.6	10.0	5.3	7.2	10.9	1.4	0.6	0.0	0.3	84.3
Percent of Property Owned by Non-Slaveholders	0.0	0.8	0.9	2.5	11.2	4.5	5.0	0.0	7.5	32.4

1860

Size of Holding	$0	$1-249	$250-499	$500-999	$1,000-4,999	$5,000-9,999	$10,000-19,999	$20,000-49,999	$50,000 and up	Totals
Percent of Population Who Were Slaveholders	1.1	0.4	0.0	0.0	0.7	2.2	1.4	3.3	2.6	11.7
Percent of Property Owned by Slaveholders	0.0	0.0	0.0	0.0	0.4	2.9	3.6	19.9	30.6	57.4
Percent of Population Who Were Non-Slaveholders	55.1	1.4	2.3	6.2	16.1	2.5	2.2	1.4	1.1	88.3
Percent of Property Owned by Non-Slaveholders	0.0	0.1	0.2	0.7	7.4	3.7	6.0	8.8	15.7	42.6

What was true of real property was also true of wealth in general in 1860. The 11.7 percent of urban family heads who owned bondsmen controlled 59.1 percent of the wealth (see table 38). On the statewide level, the 27.3 percent of all Texas families who owned slaves held 78.3

TABLE 38

DISTRIBUTION OF WEALTH AMONG SLAVEHOLDERS AND NON-SLAVEHOLDERS

IN LARGE TEXAS TOWNS, 1860

Size of Holding	$0	$1-249	$250-499	$500-999	$1,000-4,999	$5,000-9,999	$10,000-19,999	$20,000-49,999	$50,000 and up	Totals
Percent of Population Who Were Slaveholders	0.4	0.0	0.0	0.0	1.1	1.1	2.2	2.9	4.0	11.7
Percent of Wealth Owned by Slaveholders	0.0	0.0	0.0	0.0	0.5	0.9	3.7	12.6	41.4	59.1
Percent of Population Who Were Non-Slave-holders	42.3	2.2	4.6	7.7	19.7	5.8	2.8	1.5	1.5	88.1
Percent of Wealth Owned by Non-Slaveholders	0.0	0.1	0.2	0.5	5.4	5.0	5.3	5.6	18.8	40.9

percent of the wealth. Thus, although slaveholders were a smaller proportion of the town population than of the state population, and although their share (as a group) of town-owned property was smaller than in Texas as a unit, still each urban slaveowner controlled a larger slice of town property than statewide slaveholders controlled of property statewide. In short, the town-based slaveowner, as an individual, had an even greater economic edge than his rural counterpart. As a group, however, the country slaveholders had considerably more power over the economy.

Birthplace, Occupation, and Economic Status

How were the factors of birthplace and occupation related to urban wealthholding? Did some occupations and birthplaces imply more wealthholding than others? Table 39 demonstrates that household heads who were natives of the upper South and the free states were disproportionately rich in terms of real estate and total wealth, whereas foreign-born family heads held less than an equal share of real property and

TABLE 39

DISTRIBUTION OF REAL PROPERTY AND WEALTH ACCORDING TO PLACE OF BIRTH IN LARGE TEXAS TOWNS, 1850 AND 1860

	1850		1860		
	Percent of Population	Percent of Real Property	Percent of Population	Percent of Real Property	Percent of Wealth
Lower South	15.9	14.7	13.5	17.6	15.3
Upper South	9.7	21.5	13.1	30.6	27.9
Free States	17.6	39.8	12.8	30.6	33.3
Foreign-Born	56.5	24.0	60.6	21.2	23.5
Unknown	0.3	0.0	0.0	0.0	0.0
Totals	100.0	100.0	100.0	100.0	100.0

wealth. Lower Southerners, on the other hand, controlled about as large a share of real estate and wealth as their share of the town population. Did these different birthplace groups tend to concentrate in any certain occupations? Table 40 indicates that upper Southerners and free-state natives (i.e., those urban dwellers who were generally wealthier than average) were overrepresented in the merchant and professional classes, whereas the foreign-born were clustered noticeably in the lower-status occupations of skilled and unskilled workers. Again, lower Southern household heads were spread among the various occupations roughly according to their share of the total urban population.

If certain birthplace groups controlled a disproportionately large share of real estate and wealth, and if those same groups tended to cluster in certain occupation categories, does it follow that those occupation categories generally owned unusually large shares of real property and wealth? Table 41 makes the circle complete and shows that certain occupations did tend to control disproportionately large slices of real estate and wealth. The merchant and professional groups' shares of real property and total wealth were two to four times larger than their share of the urban population. The reverse was true of skilled tradesmen and unskilled workers. They constituted nearly two-thirds of the urban household heads but controlled only about 10 to 15 percent of the real property and wealth.

TABLE 40

DISTRIBUTION OF OCCUPATIONS ACCORDING TO PLACE OF BIRTH:

LARGE TEXAS TOWNS, 1850 AND 1860

(In Percentages)

	1850					1860				
	Percent of General Population	Merchants	Professions	Skilled Tradesmen	Services	Percent of General Population	Merchants	Professions	Skilled Tradesmen	Services
Lower South	15.9	9.5	15.0	6.8	31.7	13.5	7.1	16.7	11.4	18.7
Upper South	9.7	16.7	17.5	3.0	6.9	13.1	16.7	41.7	5.7	5.0
Free States	17.6	40.5	25.0	13.5	8.9	12.8	26.2	20.8	6.8	5.0
Foreign-Born	56.5	33.3	42.5	76.7	52.5	60.6	50.0	20.8	76.1	71.3
Unknown	0.3	0.0	0.0	0.0	0.0	0.0	0.0	0.0	0.0	0.0
Totals	100.0	100.0	100.0	100.0	100.0	100.0	100.0	100.0	100.0	100.0

Foreign-born family heads, because they made up such a large proportion of the town population, and merchants, because they controlled such a large percentage of urban wealth, deserve special attention. According to our sample, foreign heads of households constituted 56.5 percent of all town family heads in 1850. But among the poorest real estate holders in 1850 (those owning less than $250 in real property), the foreign-born were overrepresented at 65.2 percent, underrepresented at 47.1 percent in the middle range ($250 to $9,999), and grossly underrepresented at 11.8 percent of the wealthiest real estate holders (those with real estate worth $10,000 or more). Thus, foreign-born family heads as a group were generally less wealthy than their American-born counterparts.

The situation was similar with regard to wealth (real and personal property combined) in 1860. While foreign-born family heads made up

TABLE 41

DISTRIBUTION OF REAL PROPERTY AND WEALTH ACCORDING TO OCCUPATION:

LARGE TEXAS TOWNS, 1850 AND 1860

	1850		1860		
	Percent of Population	Percent of Real Property	Percent of Population	Percent of Real Property	Percent of Wealth
Farmers	2.5	1.2	5.5	5.9	5.3
Merchants	11.7	40.7	15.3	38.1	44.7
All Other Commerce	3.9	9.1	2.2	10.2	9.8
Professionals	11.1	22.1	8.8	24.6	20.5
Public Officials	2.2	9.3	2.2	3.4	2.9
Manufacturers	0.7	0.6	0.7	3.4	4.9
Skilled Tradesmen	37.0	8.0	32.1	6.9	5.3
Unskilled Services	28.1	7.5	29.2	3.4	3.5
Miscellaneous	2.8	1.5	4.0	4.1	3.1
Totals	100.0	100.0	100.0	100.0	100.0

60.6 percent of the urban population in 1860, they constituted 72.8 percent of the poorest urban wealthholders (those with less than $500 of real and personal estate), 55.9 percent of the middle group ($500 to $19,999), and only 18.5 percent of the richest wealthholders (more than $20,000). Again in 1860, then, foreign-born family heads tended to be less wealthy than their American-born fellow Texans, although they did make some small progress in the 1850's.

An important group in any antebellum American town were the merchants. As expected from the figures in the tables above, merchants in Texas towns controlled more property than their numbers would indicate. In 1850 merchants (i.e., those in the commercial category who called themselves "merchants" in the census returns) constituted 11.7 percent of the urban family heads; they made up only 6.8 percent of the poorest real estate holders (those with less than $250 in real property) and 14.9 percent of the middle group ($250 to $9,999), but they were greatly overrepresented in the wealthiest urban circles ($10,000 or more) at 52.9

percent. Thus, Texas merchants of 1850 were wealthier than the average town dweller, and more than half of the very richest men in the four urban centers were merchants.

The merchants' high wealth status remained about the same in 1860. On the eve of the Civil War they made up 15.3 percent of all town family heads, a slight increase over the 11.7 percent of 1850. Once again, they were clearly underrepresented in the poorest group (those with less than $500 of real and personal estate combined), slightly overrepresented in the middle range ($500 to $19,999), and greatly overrepresented in the highest wealth bracket ($20,000 or more). Merchants, then, were among the elite of Texas urban wealthholders in both 1850 and 1860.

Upper Southern and free-state natives were more likely to be rich than the foreign-born or lower Southern family heads. In addition, upper Southerners and free-state household heads were more likely to be found in the higher-status, higher-wealthholding occupations of the commercial and professional classes than were other urban birthplace groups. Finally, foreign-born Texans generally owned less than an equal share of real property and wealth, whereas merchants controlled a disproportionately large slice of real estate and total wealth.

Summary

In summary, all forms of property in both 1850 and 1860 were more unequally distributed in Texas towns than in the state as a whole, a situation comparable to that for Milwaukee County and Wisconsin in 1860 as demonstrated by Lee Soltow in his study of wealthholding in Wisconsin.[7] In addition, the trend from 1850 to 1860 in Texas towns was in favor of slightly more concentration. Urban slaveholders, though fewer and generally smaller than those statewide, held a disproportionately large share of all forms of property in both years. Foreign-born family heads, on the other hand, owned much less property than their numbers called for, whereas merchants owned considerably more than their numbers would

[7]Lee Soltow, *Patterns of Wealthholding in Wisconsin since 1850*, pp. 28-34.

seem to indicate. In short, wealth in antebellum Texas towns was generally controlled by a very small group of families, especially the American-born, slaveholders, and merchants.

Chapter 7.

Wealthholding and Political Power

THIS investigation of wealthholding among the general population, of the distribution of agricultural property and production, and of urban wealthholding has demonstrated a high degree of economic inequality in antebellum Texas. This does not, however, necessarily prove anything about the aristocratic or democratic nature of Texas politics in this period. Although often combined and confused in historical writing, questions of economic equality or inequality and political democracy or aristocracy are separate and distinct issues. The question now becomes: did the economic elite dominate political life during the 1850's?

Historians have long disputed the nature of political leadership in the antebellum South. Their debate hinges on whether or not politics in the Old South were essentially democratic or aristocratic. The view of antebellum politics as the province of an elite slaveholding class — originally associated with critics of the slave system, such as John E. Cairnes, Hinton R. Helper, and northern abolitionists — found forceful expression in the works of influential historians in the late nineteenth century. James Ford Rhodes, for example, described the political system of the Old South as a "[slaveholding] oligarchy under the republican forms." This idea appears repeatedly in twentieth-century historical literature, sometimes largely by implication, as in the writings of Ulrich B. Phillips, who emphasized slaveholder-planter domination of the Old South's economy and society. And at other times it is stated very explicitly, as in the work of Eugene Genovese, who wrote that "the planters commanded Southern politics and set the tone of social life. Theirs was an aristocratic... spirit...."[1]

The aristocratic interpretation of Southern politics has never gained total acceptance among historians. Two notable scholars who insisted on the democratic nature of Southern political life, Fletcher M. Green and Frank L. Owsley, published important works on this question in the mid-1940's. Writing in the *Journal of Southern History,* Green concluded that "by 1860 the aristocratic planter class had been shorn of its special privileges and political power. It...no longer dominated and controlled the political order." Furthermore, Green contended that with a few exceptions "the southern state governments were as democratic in 1860 as their northern sister states." Owsley, although he paid only passing attention to political affairs, insisted that "whatever influence the planters exercised over the political action of the common people... was based upon the respect the plain folk of a community had for the character and judgment of individual planters...." In short, aristocrats may have held office, but they were democratically chosen.[2]

Both interpretations are in a sense correct, and both provide valuable insights into antebellum Southern politics. There are, however, three problems with the historiographical debate as it has developed to this point. First, there has been a tendency in both schools, possibly unintentional, to oversimplify the issue. Each in seeking to make its point has been inclined to place too much emphasis on either aristocracy or democracy and thus establish a false dichotomy. Second, historians in the two schools have often reached their conclusions while analyzing different

[1]John E. Cairnes, *The Slave Power: Its Character, Career, and Probable Designs, Being an Attempt to Explain the Real Issues Involved in the American Contest,* pp 101-103; James Ford Rhodes, *History of the United States from the Compromise of 1850 to . . . 1877,* I, 345; Ulrich B. Phillips, *American Negro Slavery: A Survey of the Supply, Employment, and Control of Negro Labor as Determined by the Plantation Regime; idem, Life and Labor in the Old South;* Eugene Genovese, *The Political Economy of Slavery,* p. 28.

[2]Fletcher M. Green, "Democracy in the Old South," *Journal of Southern History* 12 (February, 1946), 23; Frank Lawrence Owsley, *Plain Folk of the Old South,* p. 139.

aspects of the same general question. Specifically, those who present the aristocratic interpretation have emphasized the practical aspect of the problem: "Who holds political power?" Proponents of the democratic view usually stress the institutional aspect: "Were there aristocratic limitations on the right to vote and the opportunity to hold office?" Third, scholars of both interpretations have not used all the evidence and research tools available; especially, they have not used quantitative methods to establish the economic status of political leaders relative to that of family heads in general. This chapter, focusing on antebellum Texas, will offer a synthesis of the aristocracy-or-democracy question; it will deal with both institutional and practical aspects of the problem; and it is based on a combination of traditional sources and quantitative methods.

By the standards of that age, the institutions of antebellum Texas provided for a democratic political system. The Texas Constitution of 1845 declared that

> every free male person who shall have attained the age of twenty-one years, and who shall be a citizen of the United States, or who is . . . a citizen of the republic of Texas, and shall have resided in this State one year next preceding an election, and the last six months within the district, county, city, or town in which he offers to vote, (Indians not taxed, Africans, and descendents of Africans, excepted,) shall be deemed a qualified elector . . . .[3]

These voters were to elect members of the state legislature, the governor, lieutenant governor, commissioner of the land office, and, after 1850, the attorney general, comptroller, and treasurer.[4] With the exception of age and residence requirements — the governor, for example, had to be at least thirty years old and a resident of the state for three years — there

[3]Texas State Constitution of 1845, in Ernest Wallace and David M. Vigness, eds., *Documents of Texas History*, pp. 149-159. The quotation is from page 150.

[4]Rupert N. Richardson, Ernest Wallace, and Adrian Anderson, *Texas: The Lone Star State*, p. 135. The democratic nature of political institutions in antebellum Texas is emphasized in a recently published analysis of southern political arrangements. See Ralph A. Wooster, *The People in Power: Courthouse and Statehouse in the Lower South, 1850-1860*, pp. 107, 116.

were no greater limitations on the right to hold office than there were on the right to vote. In short, there were no aristocratic restrictions on voting or officeholding; neither voters nor officeholders had to meet property or tax-paying qualifications.

Thus, the Constitution of 1845 provided for free adult male suffrage. The next question is whether there were extraconstitutional restrictions on the franchise; that is, did an aristocratic class employ economic coercion or physical intimidation to control elections in antebellum Texas? Although such methods are hardly unknown in American political history, there is simply no evidence that Texas voters in the prewar period were coerced or intimidated when exercising their right to vote.[5]

It is relatively simple to establish who was eligible to vote and hold office in antebellum Texas, and it seems certain that there were no extralegal restrictions on the suffrage. But a more difficult question remains: who actually exercised political power? That is, what was the economic status of the people who led political parties and held public office? At this point we move from the institutional to the practical aspect of the issue.

Identification of Political Leaders

Since the best source of information on the social and economic background of antebellum Texans in general is the United States censuses of 1850 and 1860, we limited this investigation to a four-year period around the date of each census (1848 to 1851 and 1858 to 1861). We assumed that individuals who were political leaders in either of these four-year periods could reasonably be expected to appear in the appropri-

[5]Generally, franchise requirements such as these would be described as "adult white male" suffrage. However, the word "white" was deliberately omitted by the Texas constitutional convention in order to prevent Mexicans from being excluded from voting (see Frederic L. Paxson, "The Constitution of Texas, 1845," *Southwestern Historical Quarterly* 18 [April, 1915], 392; Annie Middleton, "The Texas Convention of 1845," *Southwestern Historical Quarterly* 25 [July, 1921], 42). Owsley, *Plain Folk of the Old South*, pp. 138-139, raised the question of coercion and also answered it negatively.

ate census. Although an individual's economic status may have changed somewhat within a year or two, we also assumed that the census provides a reasonably accurate picture of these leaders' economic circumstances at the time they wielded power.

We defined "political leaders" as follows: all elected federal officeholders (representatives and senators); all elected state officials (governor, lieutenant governor, attorney general, treasurer, comptroller, commissioner of the general land office, members of the state legislature, and the secretary of state, who was appointed); delegates to the secession convention of 1861; political party leaders (officials of the Democratic state conventions in 1848, 1852, and 1860 and the Whig state convention of 1852); and the most important elected officials on the county level, chief justices and county commissioners. In the case of county leaders, due to the large number of counties involved (105 in 1860), we took a sample by arranging the counties in random order and analyzing the leaders for every other county.[6]

[6]The names of state officeholders were obtained from *The Texas Almanac and State Industrial Guide, 1970-1971,* pp. 635-638; names of federal officeholders were obtained from *Biographical Directory of the American Congress, 1774-1949,* pp. 231, 238, 270. Names of members of the state legislature were obtained from *Members of the Texas Legislature, 1846-1962,* pp. 9-12, 32-36 (this study was limited to those individuals in the legislatures of 1849-1851 and 1859-1861 because the service of these officials spanned the census years 1850 and 1860, and therefore, they were more likely to be located in the census). Names of delegates to the secession convention were obtained from Ralph A. Wooster, "An Analysis of the Membership of the Texas Secession Convention," *Southwestern Historical Quarterly* 62 (January, 1959), 328-335 (though not legally elected officials or party leaders, members of the convention may correctly be considered as important political leaders). Names of party leaders were obtained from Ernest William Winkler, ed., *Platforms of Political Parties in Texas,* pp. 44, 49-54, 81-85 (because it was desirable to identify as many party leaders as possible, the Democratic and Whig state conventions of 1852 were included, even though they fell just outside our years of investigation). Names of chief justices and county commissioners were obtained from Records of the Secretary of State, Election Registers, 1846-1854 and 1854-1861 (Archives Division, Texas State Library, Austin). Wooster *(The People in Power),* using many of these same sources, compiled information on state and county officeholders and compared them with similar officials in other lower South states.

Once we had compiled the names of all these political leaders, we attempted to locate each individual in the manuscript returns of the appropriate United States census. For the 1848-1851 period we identified 360 (85.9 percent) of the 419 leaders whose names we had compiled. For the 1858-1861 period we found 643 (83.4 percent) of 771 individuals.[7] Once we had located them in the census, we took information for each on age, occupation, birthplace, real and personal property, slaveholding, and agricultural property and production. These data were punched onto IBM cards and processed with the aid of a computer.

At this point it should be emphasized that we dealt with all levels of political leadership from national to county, not just with the higher echelons where wealth is often considered a prerequisite for office. In 1850 the 360 leaders were distributed among the following groups: 71.7 percent were from the county level; 19.7 percent were from the state level; 6.7 percent were political party leaders; and 1.9 percent, including all the federal officeholders identified, held office on more than one of these levels. Ten years later, 58 percent were from the local level, 36.4 percent were state officials, 3 percent were party officers, 2.5 percent held office on more than one level, and one person (0.1 percent) served at the federal level alone. Thus, because a majority of those examined in both 1850 and 1860 occupied grassroots political positions, our measurements of wealthholding among political leaders in antebellum Texas are not biased upward by undue emphasis on holders of the highest federal and state offices.

The data collected provided a statistical profile of the economic status of antebellum Texas' political leaders. This information is relatively meaningless, however, unless it is compared with a similar profile of the state's heads of households in 1850 and 1860, that is, unless it is put in context. The necessary context is provided by our samples from the 1850 and 1860 manuscript censuses.

Tables 42 and 43 break down the sample populations and the political

[7]The 419 leaders in 1850 and 771 in 1860 were those for whom home counties could be determined. There were a few whose home counties could not be ascertained.

TABLE 42

SLAVEHOLDING-OCCUPATIONAL STATUS OF SAMPLE POPULATION AND POLITICAL LEADERS, 1850

(In Percentages)

	Whole State		Region I		Region II		Region III		Region IV	
	Sample Population	Leaders	Sample Population	Leaders	Sample Population	Leaders	Sample Population	Leaders	Sample Population	Leaders
Slaveholding Farmers with Farms	23.8	41.4	28.6	46.9	22.1	34.4	16.4	24.6	20.3	48.4
Slaveholding Farmers without Farms	2.0	2.5	3.5	1.4	1.0	8.2	0.4	0.0	1.0	2.2
Non-Slaveholding Farmers with Farms	38.9	23.9	39.9	23.8	18.2	4.9	62.6	57.4	31.7	13.4
Non-Slaveholding Farmers without Farms	12.7	3.6	15.6	3.4	8.7	3.3	12.0	1.6	9.6	5.5
Slaveholding Non-Farmers	4.3	14.4	3.5	9.5	9.9	26.2	0.7	6.6	5.1	19.8
Non-Slaveholding Non-Farmers	18.3	14.2	8.9	15.0	40.1	23.0	7.9	9.8	32.3	10.7
Totals	100.0	100.0	100.0	100.0	100.0	100.0	100.0	100.0	100.0	100.0

TABLE 43

SLAVEHOLDING-OCCUPATIONAL STATUS OF SAMPLE POPULATION AND POLITICAL LEADERS, 1860

(In Percentages)

	Whole State		Region I		Region II		Region III		Region IV	
	Sample Population	Leaders	Sample Population	Leaders	Sample Population	Leaders	Sample Population	Leaders	Sample Population	Leaders
Slaveholding Farmers with Farms	22.7	51.1	29.8	58.1	17.4	47.5	16.8	41.1	20.3	52.3
Slaveholding Farmers without Farms	1.3	3.4	1.3	3.6	1.1	6.4	1.4	1.8	1.1	2.6
Non-Slaveholding Farmers with Farms	37.4	17.4	39.1	12.5	12.1	12.8	44.2	31.9	36.3	12.4
Non-Slaveholding Farmers without Farms	13.0	4.2	11.6	2.0	2.7	2.6	19.7	6.8	11.2	5.9
Slaveholding Non-Farmers	3.3	13.8	3.3	17.3	10.1	19.2	1.6	8.6	2.7	11.1
Non-Slaveholding Non-Farmers	22.3	10.1	14.9	6.5	56.6	11.5	16.3	9.8	28.4	15.7
Totals	100.0	100.0	100.0	100.0	100.0	100.0	100.0	100.0	100.0	100.0

leaders of antebellum Texas according to slaveholding-occupational status for the whole state and for all four regions in both 1850 and 1860. In a predominantly non-slaveholding society, slaveowners dominated the ranks of political leaders. In 1850, when slaveholders were only 30.1 percent of the sample, they constituted 58.3 percent of the political leaders. Ten years later the situation was even more striking. Slaveholders provided 68.3 percent of the leaders in spite of the fact that they were only 27.3 percent of the statewide sample. The tables also indicate that slaveholding farmers constituted a much larger proportion of the state's political leaders than they did of heads of households in both 1850 and 1860. Indeed, in 1860 slaveholding farmers were a majority of the political leaders, although they were less than one quarter of the sample population. On the other hand, non-slaveholding farmers, who made up more than 50 percent of all heads of households in both census years, provided only about one-fourth of the political leaders. Among non-farmers, slaveowners constituted a much greater proportion of the political leaders than they did of the sample population.

The same general situation emerges for the four regions of antebellum Texas. Only region III, the more frontier area of Texas in the 1850's, varied appreciably in its political leadership from the pattern of dominance by slaveholders. Even there, in 1850 and especially by 1860, slaveowners held a disproportionately large share of the positions of public leadership. Although slaveholders constituted only 17.5 percent of the heads of households there in 1850, they accounted for 31.2 percent of the political leaders. Ten years later slaveholders had increased to 19.8 percent of all heads of households; their share of public offices had advanced much more rapidly to 51.5 percent of the total. In fact, on the eve of the Civil War, slaveholders provided a majority of the political leaders in all four regions of Texas.

Table 44 compares the wealthholding of the sample population and of leaders in four important categories. In 1850 slaveholding leaders owned, on the average, slightly more slaves than did slaveholders in our sample statewide. In addition, leaders in 1850 averaged more than four times as

TABLE 44

MEAN PROPERTY HOLDINGS IN ANTEBELLUM TEXAS: SAMPLE POPULATION AND POLITICAL LEADERS

1850

	Whole State		Region I		Region II		Region III		Region IV	
	Sample Population	Leaders	Sample Population	Leaders	Sample Population	Leaders	Sample Population	Leaders	Sample Population	Leaders
Number of Slaves*	7.2	8.8	6.9	9.6	10.9	9.6	4.4	3.8	6.5	8.6
Value of Real Property	$ 1,461	$ 6,503	$ 1,082	$ 6,702	$ 2,985	$ 6,644	$ 910	$ 1,808	$ 1,727	$ 9,237

1860

	Sample Population	Leaders	Population	Leaders	Sample Population	Leaders	Sample Population	Leaders	Sample Population	Leaders
Number of Slaves*	9.4	14.9	9.9	15.3	14.3	20.6	5.9	9.4	9.4	15.3
Value of Real Property	$ 2,699	$12,646	$ 2,238	$ 9,575	$ 6,722	$24,762	$ 1,189	$ 7,065	$ 2,865	$17,316
Value of Personal Property	3,692	12,829	4,272	14,483	5,926	17,975	2,200	7,562	3,651	13,105
Wealth	6,393	25,499	6,516	24,058	12,648	43,144	4,110	14,627	6,516	30,422

*In the case of slave property, the averages are for slaveholders only, not for the entire sample population.

much real property as did the sample population. The disparities in wealthholding between the two groups were at least as pronounced in 1860. In real and personal property holdings and in wealth (a combination of real and personal estate), political leaders owned roughly four times as much as heads of household in the sample population. Where slaveholdings were concerned, political leaders averaged 14.9 bondsmen each, 59 percent more than slaveowners statewide.[8]

An examination of wealthholding in the four geographical regions demonstrates a consistent increase from 1850 to 1860 in the advantage leaders enjoyed over family heads in general. In 1850, although the average slaveholding varied from region to region, the holdings of leaders and all household heads were roughly comparable in each region. In the case of real property, political leaders had a more distinct advantage, averaging from two to six times as much real estate as did heads of of households statewide. By 1860, although the average size of slaveholdings still varied from region to region, the holdings of political leaders were substantially larger in every region. Where real estate, personal property, and wealth in total were concerned, political leaders in 1860 owned on the average three to seven times as much as did family heads in the sample population. Thus, although the situation varied somewhat from one geographical area of Texas to another, during the 1850's political leaders enjoyed an economic status far superior to that of the population statewide.

As tables 42 and 43 illustrated, roughly three-fourths of the sample population and of the political leaders were farmers. Thus, any comparison of the economic circumstances of these two groups must deal with key elements of agricultural property and production. Table 45 indicates that in 1850 political leaders who operated farms enjoyed a substantial advantage in the average number of improved acres, cash value of farms, bushels of corn, and bales of cotton. Ten years later their advantage was even greater, two to three times as much as the average for the sample

[8]All these mean figures, for the sample population and for the leaders, were accompanied by high standard deviations. The standard deviations for the means of leaders' holdings were smaller than those for the mean holdings of the sample, indicating a smaller range of variation in the holdings of political leaders.

TABLE 45

MEAN HOLDINGS IN AGRICULTURAL PROPERTY AND PRODUCTION AMONG ANTEBELLUM TEXAS FARM OPERATORS: SAMPLE POPULATION AND POLITICAL LEADERS

1850

	Whole State		Region I		Region II		Region III		Region IV	
	Sample Population	Leaders	Sample Population	Leaders	Sample Population	Leaders	Sample Population	Leaders	Sample Population	Leaders
Number of Improved Acres	42.0	74.1	46.1	81.2	56.3	88.6	27.5	41.5	40.5	83.7
Cash Value of Farm	$ 1,138	$ 3,041	$ 1,000	$ 3,045	$ 2,345	$ 4,125	$ 747	$ 977	$ 1,390	$ 4,387
Number of Bushels of Corn	400.0	789.2	376.6	612.3	667.1	1,156.2	280.4	502.7	474.4	1,208.9
Number of Bales of Cotton	3.3	6.7	3.2	6.0	8.4	14.8	0.5	0.4	4.2	10.0

1860

	Sample Population	Leaders	Sample Population	Leaders	Sample Population	Leaders	Sample Population	Leaders	Sample Population	Leaders
Number of Improved Acres	66.5	176.3	73.6	177.8	125.9	187.2	46.6	102.4	66.2	256.6
Cash Value of Farm	$ 2,749	$ 9,060	$ 2,061	$ 6,142	$10,027	$16,917	$ 2,315	$ 6,611	$ 3,198	$13,328
Number of Bushels of Corn	417.2	960.5	499.3	1,081.2	1,117.9	1,308.6	258.2	612.5	321.1	993.3
Number of Bales of Cotton	10.4	32.5	13.1	34.4	35.8	71.3	1.4	7.9	11.4	39.6

population. Especially striking are the figures on cotton, the most important cash crop in the state's agricultural economy. In 1850 political leaders produced, on the average, twice as much cotton as farm operators in general. By 1860 this advantage was even greater, with leaders producing more than three times as much as farm operators statewide.

In the four geographical regions political leaders enjoyed an advantage in virtually every category of agricultural property and production in both census years. East Texas (region I) and south-central Texas (region IV) conformed closely to the state pattern both in mean size of holdings and in the degree of advantage held by leaders. Interestingly, coastal Texas (region II), where the mean property holdings were considerably larger than holdings statewide, and north-central Texas (region III), where these means were smaller, had the smallest disparities between the holdings of political leaders and the sample family heads. In region II, this situation may be explained by the high percentage of large farmers in the general agricultural population; their large holdings doubtless raised the means for all. In region III, the absence of large planters probably accounts for the smaller disparities between the holdings of political leaders and farmers in general. By 1860, however, as this frontier region matured economically, the advantage enjoyed by political leaders increased to a point more comparable to that for leaders statewide.

Characteristics of Political Leaders

In practice, then, political leadership in antebellum Texas was provided primarily by an economic elite, people who were generally two to four times richer than the population in general in terms of all important aspects of wealthholding. Were there other characteristics, in addition to greater wealthholding, that distinguished political leaders from the general population, and if so, do these characteristics explain the economic advantage enjoyed by these leaders? Obviously, a comparison of such factors as age, occupation, and birthplace cannot fully explain political domination or disparities in wealthholding between the two groups. But a comparative profile of leaders and the general population may suggest some of the elements involved in rising to political leadership in Texas during the 1850's.

In the first place, political leaders and heads of households in general did differ slightly in terms of age. Leaders were on the average three years older in both 1850 and 1860. Since individuals tended to accumulate wealth as they aged, this small age differential probably did account for part of the disparity in wealthholding between political leaders and family heads in general.

Table 46 compares the birthplaces of political leaders with those of heads of households in the population as a whole. It reveals that in both 1850 and 1860 natives of the upper South provided a disproportionately large share of political leadership. Indeed, even though they declined as a percentage of the total population from 1850 to 1860, upper Southerners constituted a majority of the leaders in both years. Perhaps upper Southerners predominated because many upper Southern families had been established longer in Texas and therefore enjoyed a position that allowed frequent participation in public affairs. The only group underrepresented in terms of political leadership were the foreign-born, who were concen-

TABLE 46

PLACES OF BIRTH OF ANTEBELLUM TEXANS: SAMPLE POPULATION AND POLITICAL LEADERS

(In Percentages)

	1850		1860	
	Sample Population	Leaders	Sample Population	Leaders
Lower South	30.2	28.3	36.0	37.0
Upper South	45.6	54.0	41.1	53.2
Free States	9.5	10.5	8.1	5.7
Foreign-Born	14.2	6.9	14.5	3.9
Unknown	0.5	0.3	0.3	0.2
Totals	100.0	100.0	100.0	100.0

trated in the large towns and who were primarily engaged in less prestigious, lower-paying occupations.[9]

Where occupations were concerned, table 47 demonstrates that, as expected for an overwhelmingly agricultural society, approximately two-thirds of the political leaders listed their primary occupation as farmer. Of the other leaders, professionals such as lawyers and doctors provided a disproportionately large share. Obviously, by definition, a similar situation was to be expected in the case of those who were public officials by occupation. On the other hand, skilled tradesmen such as carpenters, shoemakers, and blacksmiths, and service occupations such as clerks, tavern keepers, and laborers were underrepresented among political leaders in both 1850 and 1860, especially in the latter year. In summary,

TABLE 47

OCCUPATIONS OF ANTEBELLUM TEXANS: SAMPLE POPULATION AND POLITICAL LEADERS

(In Percentages)

	1850		1860	
	Sample Population	Leaders	Sample Population	Leaders
Farmers*	71.3	62.5	69.7	65.2
Merchants	3.8	6.7	4.3	4.7
Professionals	5.4	15.8	5.0	21.9
Public Officials	0.7	5.8	0.8	4.5
Manufacturers	1.1	0.6	1.1	0.3
Skilled Tradesmen	10.9	5.8	9.2	1.7
Services	5.8	2.8	9.2	0.9
Misc. & Unknown	1.0	0.0	0.7	0.8
Totals	100.0	100.0	100.0	100.0

* The percentages of farmers in this table are slightly smaller than the percentages for farmers given on page 66. This slight discrepancy results from the fact that some individuals, although they owned farms, reported themselves to the census taker by another primary occupation. Since this table is a detailed occupational breakdown, it reports the occupation as listed in the manuscript census.

9See chapter 6.

political leaders were concentrated among the wealthier class of farmers (as explained above) and among the more prestigious, higher-paying non-farm occupations. Occupation, then, was an important element involved in rising to political leadership. But in the case of farming, the principal occupation of antebellum Texans, occupation was obviously less important than financial success.

Thus, the typical political leader in Texas during the 1850's was most likely to be much wealthier than the average Texan, a slaveholder (unlike the average Texan), a larger slaveholder than average, a native of the upper South, and a large farmer or a professional. In short, wealthy slaveholders dominated political leadership in antebellum Texas.

Summary

Our evidence suggests that, in the case of Texas at least, both interpretations of antebellum Southern politics are valid to an extent. There was democracy, for Texas had no property or tax-paying restrictions on voting or officeholding; legally, any free adult male could vote or hold political office.[10] And there was aristocracy, for a very high proportion of those who actually wielded political power at all levels of government were members of the slaveholding economic elite. Thus, the politics of antebellum Texas were a synthesis of aristocracy and democracy.

How did Texas compare with other areas of the United States before the Civil War in terms of the democratic-aristocratic question? Were Texas and the South aristocratic enclaves in a democratic republic? The few systematic investigations that deal precisely with these questions indicate that wealthy aristocracies wielded political power in other areas of the antebellum United States much as they did in Texas. Lee Soltow's

[10]Free Negroes and untaxed Indians were exceptions to this rule. In general, however, Indians were not citizens in the United States, and there were very few free blacks in Texas — 397 in 1850 and 355 in 1860, including men, women, and children (J. D. B. DeBow, ed., *Statistical View of the United States, Being a Compendium of the Seventh Census*, p. 83; U.S. Bureau of the Census, *Eighth Census of the United States, Population*, p. 486).

study of wealthholding in Wisconsin, for example, found that the average Wisconsin state senator in 1860 was 9.3 times wealthier than the average adult male. The economic advantage enjoyed by Wisconsin state senators was much greater than that enjoyed by Texas political leaders in general. Edward Pessen's work on wealth and power in major northeastern cities before the Civil War, although it does not specifically measure wealth differences between political leaders and the general population, clearly indicates that an aristocratic, wealthy elite dominated the urban northeast economically, politically, and socially. Indeed, scholars investigating social class and political power in a number of widely scattered towns and cities in the antebellum North and West have found similar domination by a wealthy elite.[11] Perhaps Fletcher Green was correct: Texas was as democratic institutionally — and practically, too, for that matter — as her Northern sister states.[12]

Politics in antebellum Texas, then, combined elements of democracy and aristocracy. Furthermore, Texas political life was not unlike political arrangements elsewhere in the antebellum United States. A systématic comparison of the economic status of political leaders with that of the general population in the contemporary United States may well reveal the same type of domination by an economic aristocracy.

[11]Lee Soltow, *Patterns of Wealthholding in Wisconsin since 1850*, pp. 146-147; Edward Pessen, *Riches, Class, and Power before the Civil War*, pp. 281-301.

[12] Only five northern states (all the New England states except Connecticut) had Negro suffrage in 1860, and they contained only 6 percent of the total northern Negro population (Leon F. Litwack, *North of Slavery: The Negro in the Free States, 1790-1860*, p. 263).

Chapter 8.

Comparisons of Wealthholding: Other Places and Other Times

ANTEBELLUM Texas was not a land of economic equality. There was a high degree of concentration in real property, personal property, slaves, and total wealth — that is, in all categories of wealthholding — among the entire free population. Indeed, a minority, constituting less than 10 percent of the total population, owned more than half of each of these forms of property in both 1850 and 1860. Among the agricultural population, which accounted for roughly three-fourths of all the state's families, a similar situation of economic inequality existed. There was a high level of concentration in all categories of farm property and production; a small group of large farmers, less than 10 percent of the total, generally controlled between one-third and one-half of improved acreage, farm value, livestock value, corn, and cotton. In the large towns of antebellum Texas wealth was even more unequally distributed than in the state as a whole or within the agricultural population.

A full perspective on the question of economic equality or inequality in antebellum Texas demands comparison not only with the situation existing in other slave states but with that in free areas during the prewar period and with that in the twentieth-century United States. How did wealthholding in Texas compare with distributions of wealth in other places and at other times? Perhaps the simpler, overwhelmingly agrarian society of antebellum Texas, in spite of its high degree of concentration in wealthholding, was more equalitarian than other more complicated or highly developed regions of the mid-nineteenth-century United States. On the other hand, it may be that Texas with its slaveholding elite was marked by greater inequality than most areas of the free states of the North. And what of the United States a century after the destruction of slavery? Perhaps federal regulation of the economy, graduated income taxes, and massive social welfare programs adopted in the more than one hundred years since the Civil War have reduced economic inequality. Conversely, decades of industrialization and urbanization may have created greater inequality in the twentieth century than existed in antebellum Texas.

Before proceeding to comparisons of wealthholding in other places and other times, we should repeat that the Gini index may be interpreted in two ways: first, in relation to the range of the statistic itself, and second, relative to other Gini indices. Thus far, we have employed the first of these methods. From this point on, we will use the second interpretation also.

Among the entire free population, wealth seems to have been even more unequally distributed in the United States as a whole in 1860 than in Texas at the same time. Robert Gallman's work, "Trends in the Size Distribution of Wealth in the Nineteenth Century," provides an estimate of wealthholding for American families in 1860. Gallman's measurement is based on sample distributions for several key states and cities taken to be representative of the United States in general. Although his estimate is not derived from a systematic national sample, it is one of the most thorough and reliable available. A comparison of his national figures and our own measurements for Texas (see table 48) reveals that Texas' level of inequality, although high, was somewhat lower than that for the nation as a whole. According to Gallman, the wealthiest 2 percent of American families controlled 35 percent of the wealth. In Texas the richest 2.2 percent owned 32.2 percent of the wealth. The Gini index of concentration for wealthholding in the entire United States in 1860 was .824; the index for Texas in 1860 was slightly lower at .742. A more recent study of wealth distribution in the United States as a whole in 1860 is provided in

Lee Soltow's *Men and Wealth in the United States.* Employing a somewhat different unit of analysis — males twenty years of age or older — Soltow found that the richest 2 percent owned 40 percent of all wealth and that the Gini index for the nation was .832. Although the difference is not great, the evidence from Gallman and Soltow indicates that antebellum Texas, even with its slaveholding elite, compared favorably with the United States as a whole in terms of economic equality.[1]

At the state level wealth distributions are available for Louisiana in the deep South, Maryland in the border states, and Wisconsin in the North. The Louisiana estimate, also derived from Gallman's work, excludes the population of New Orleans. Large cities like New Orleans invariably raise the level of wealth concentration for a state. Since Texas had no cities even remotely comparable in size to New Orleans, Gallman's measurements for Louisiana excluding New Orleans are especially suitable for our comparisons. Table 48 indicates that the degree of economic inequality in Louisiana was closely comparable to that in the nation as a whole and therefore slightly greater than that in Texas in 1860. In Louisiana the richest 2 percent of all families controlled 37.3 percent of all wealth (compared with 2.2 percent owning 32.2 percent in Texas and 2 percent owning 35 percent in the whole country). The Gini index for Louisiana (.826) was almost identical to that for the United States (.824) and was somewhat higher than the index for Texas (.742).[2] Thus, Louisia-

[1]Robert E. Gallman, "Trends in the Size Distribution of Wealth in the Nineteenth Century: Some Speculations," in Lee Soltow, ed., *Six Papers on the Size Distribution of Wealth and Income,* pp. 1-25; Lee Soltow, *Men and Wealth in the United States, 1850-1870,* pp. 99, 103. A sample based on adult males may produce a Gini index slightly higher than a sample of the same population based on heads of households, but the difference would probably not be great. In any case, we used heads of households as our unit of measurement because it seemed to be the most logical approach to the problem. The overwhelming majority of households consisted of a single family, and single families were the most meaningful wealthholding units. In addition, most measurements of antebellum wealthholding utilize heads of households as the sampling unit.

[2]Gallman, "Size Distribution of Wealth in the Nineteenth Century," pp. 22-23.

TABLE 48

INDICATORS OF WEALTHHOLDING, 1860

	Texas	United States (Gallman)	United States (Soltow)**	Louisiana	Maryland	Wisconsin**
Percent of Wealth Owned by Richest 2 Percent*	32.2	35.0	40.0	37.3	25.8	31.0
Gini Index	.742	.824	.832	.826	.795	.752

* 2.2 percent in the case of Texas

** Soltow's calculation is based on a sample of males twenty years of age and over, slightly different from our sample of heads of households.

na's wealth was slightly more concentrated than wealth in Texas, possibly due to the presence of numerous huge sugar plantations in Louisiana.

Maryland, excluding the large city of Baltimore, was taken by Gallman as representative of the border states in 1860. As table 48 indicates, the degree of concentration there (.795) was slightly greater than that for Texas (.742). Interestingly, the richest 2 percent of Marylanders controlled 25.8 percent of the wealth, a smaller share than was owned by the richest 2 percent in either the United States or Texas.[3] However, because wealth was so unequally distributed among the rest of the state's population, Maryland's overall level of concentration was quite comparable to those for the United States and Texas.

The northern state of Wisconsin has been the subject of intensive study by Lee Soltow, who published his findings in *Patterns of Wealthholding in Wisconsin since 1850.* His findings reveal that the distribution of wealth in Wisconsin — a northwestern state highly comparable to Texas in terms of length of statehood, proximity to the frontier, and total population — was remarkably similar to the distribution for Texas. The richest 2 percent of Wisconsin's adult males owned 31 percent of the wealth, very near the 32.2 percent figure for Texas. In addition, the Gini

[3]*Ibid.*

indices for the two states (.742 for Texas and .752 for Wisconsin) are nearly identical.[4]

In summary, the levels of economic inequality in 1860 in the United States as a whole, in Texas, Louisiana, and Maryland, and in Wisconsin were closely comparable. Actually, the degree of concentration was slightly lower in Texas. Thus, the generally accepted idea that wealth was more unequally distributed in the slave South than in the northern states is not borne out by the situation in Texas. Certainly, wealth distributions varied from one slave state to another, as the comparisons of Texas, Louisiana, and Maryland indicate, but the general conclusion must be that wealth was at least as equally distributed in the South as in the North, perhaps more so.

The major new quantitative work on the economics of Negro slavery by Robert W. Fogel and Stanley L. Engerman, although it does not investigate the questions of wealthholding in any detail, does suggest that wealth was no more concentrated in the slave South than in the North. Fogel and Engerman reasoned that (1) the distribution of wealth was much more unequal in urban than in rural areas; (2) the distribution of wealth was slightly more unequal in the rural South than in the rural North; and (3) the overall inequality of the wealth distribution was roughly the same in the South as in the North, since the greater weight of the urban population in the North offset the higher level of inequality in the rural South.[5] Obviously, the first statement holds true in virtually all cases. In order to test the second statement, we compared the level of concentration in wealthholding for rural Wisconsin (excluding Milwaukee) and the level for rural Texas (excluding Galveston, Houston, San Antonio, and Austin) in 1860. The Gini index for rural Wisconsin was .72;

[4]Lee Soltow, *Patterns of Wealthholding in Wisconsin since 1850*, pp. 5, 45. Furthermore, Gini indices for real estate in 1850 in the two states were also very similar: .77 in Wisconsin and .78 in Texas (*ibid.*, 9).

[5]Robert William Fogel and Stanley L. Engerman, *Time on the Cross: The Economics of American Negro Slavery*, II, 165.

that for rural Texas was virtually identical at .73.[6] Thus, if wealth in the rural South was not noticeably more concentrated than it was in the rural North, the greater proportion of the northern population that was urban probably meant an overall higher level of wealth concentration in the antebellum North than in the South.

Another type of comparison, especially important for an overwhelmingly agrarian society like Texas, is one based on agricultural property and production. In this case, the best source of information for the purpose of comparison is a recent article by Gavin Wright in *Agricultural History*. Drawing data from manuscript census samples of the major cotton-producing counties in the South in 1850 and 1860, Wright computed indices of concentration for the "Cotton South" on improved acreage, cash value of farm, cotton, and slaves owned by farm operators.[7] Table 49 compares the indices for Texas and for the Cotton South and reveals moderate to high levels of concentration in all cases. In Texas the degrees of concentration in improved acreage and cash value of farms were slightly lower than those for the Cotton South in both 1850 and 1860. Perhaps this situation is explained by the availability of much cheap land in the more recently settled state of Texas. The indices for cotton and agricultural slaves in Texas in both census years, on the other hand, were somewhat higher than those for the Cotton South. This circumstance seems curious; however, its explanation probably lies in the relatively less developed state of Texas' agricultural economy. Where there are a few

[6]Soltow, *Patterns of Wealthholding in Wisconsin*, p. 66, presents information on rural Wisconsin (excluding Milwaukee). Although there were numerous small towns with populations in the 1,000-2,000 range included in Soltow's "rural Wisconsin," this fact does not weaken our comparison because we too included small towns in rural Texas, and those Texas towns considered to be urban were larger than the Wisconsin towns except Milwaukee.

[7]Gavin Wright, " 'Economic Democracy' and the Concentration of Agricultural Wealth in the Cotton South, 1850-1860," *Agricultural History* 44 (January, 1970), 63-93. The "Cotton South," as defined in Wright's article, consisted of 382 cotton-producing counties that accounted for 93 percent of all cotton grown in the United States in 1859. Wright's work is based on a sample of 5,229 "Cotton South" farms selected under the direction of Robert E. Gallman and William N. Parker.

TABLE 49

GINI INDICES FOR AGRICULTURAL PROPERTY AND PRODUCTION, 1850 AND 1860

	1850				1860			
	Improved Acreage	Cash Value of Farm	Cotton	Agricultural Slaves	Improved Acreage	Cash Value of Farm	Cotton	Agricultural Slaves
Texas	.502	.611	.883	.821	.548	.645	.852	.828
Cotton South	.571	.698	.713	.723	.575	.678	.730	.747

large slaveholding cotton producers and many small ones, as in Texas in the 1850's, the indices of concentration will be higher than in an area where there are relatively more large slaveowning cotton growers and fewer small producers, as in the Cotton South as a whole in the 1850's. (This can be demonstrated by comparing the Gini index on cotton production for region I in 1850 with the index for the same area in 1860. In 1850, when the region had relatively few large producers and many small ones, the Gini index was .864. By 1860, when region I contained relatively more large growers and fewer small ones, the Gini index dropped to .811.) Had the slaveholding, cotton-producing regime continued through the 1860's and 1870's, it is likely that levels of concentration in agricultural property and production would have stabilized near those for the Cotton South as a whole.

It is generally understood that wealth was more unequally distributed in large cities than in rural areas. Does this conclusion hold true even for such relatively small towns as Galveston, Houston, San Antonio, and Austin? Furthermore, how did the urban areas of Texas compare with cities in other areas of the antebellum United States in terms of wealthholding?

As demonstrated in chapter 6, real estate, personal property, and total wealth were more highly concentrated in the towns of Galveston, Houston, San Antonio, and (by 1860) Austin than in the state as a whole. The Gini index for real estate in 1850 was .868 for the town populations compared with .780 for Texas as a whole; in 1860 the urban index (.863) was still higher than the statewide figure (.786). The indices for personal property in 1860 (.894 for the towns and .756 for the state) and wealth in 1860 (.849 for the towns and .742 for the state) demonstrate the same relationship. Thus, even in these relatively small towns of antebellum Texas wealth was more unequally distributed than in rural areas of the Lone Star state.

Patterns of wealthholding in antebellum Texas towns may also be compared with those in major cities in other areas of the United States. Among the cities of the slave South, the information necessary for comparisons is available for New Orleans in the deep South and Baltimore and St. Louis in the border states (see table 50). In all three cities the Gini indices and the shares of wealth held by the richest 1, 2, and 5 percent of the families were greater than those for the large towns of Texas. It seems that concentration tended to increase as a city became older, larger, and more complex.[8]

Among Northern cities the same general pattern emerges: those for which reasonably precise comparisons can be made exhibited higher degrees of concentration than did urban areas in Texas. Milwaukee, a northwestern city of 45,246 people located in a state roughly the age of Texas, had a slightly higher level of concentration overall and considerably more wealth controlled by the richest 1 percent of its families. Four major northeastern cities — Brooklyn, Boston, New York, and Philadelphia — also displayed higher degrees of wealth concentration than did the large towns of Texas.[9] Thus, wealthholding in Texas towns,

[8]Gallman, "Size Distribution of Wealth in the Nineteenth Century," pp. 22-23.

[9]Soltow, *Patterns of Wealthholding in Wisconsin*, p. 5; Milwaukee's total population is from *Eighth Census of the United States, 1860, Population*, p. 539. Edward Pessen's estimate of wealth concentration for Philadelphia, (*Riches, Class, and Power before the Civil War*,

TABLE 50

INDICATORS OF WEALTHHOLDING FOR URBAN POPULATION BY FAMILY

	Texas Towns*	New Orleans	Baltimore	St. Louis	Milwaukee	Brooklyn	Boston	New York	Philadelphia
Gini Index	.849	.886	.898	.878	.893	.865	.862	NA	NA
Percent of Wealth Held by Richest 1%	21.3	43.0	38.5	37.6	44.0	42.0	37.0	40.0	50.0
Percent of Wealth Held by Richest 2%	33.9	56.6	53.5	50.2	NA	NA	NA	NA	NA
Percent of Wealth Held by Richest 5%	58.0	71.6	71.7	67.7	NA	NA	NA	NA	NA

Note: All figures are for 1860 except those for Brooklyn (1841), Boston (1848), and New York (1845). Figures for Milwaukee, taken from Soltow, Patterns of Wealthholding, are based on adult males, not family heads, as mentioned above. Figures for other non-Texas cities are from Gallman, "Size Distribution of Wealth in the Nineteenth Century." NA = not available.

* For Texas the wealthiest 1.1 percent, 2.2 percent, and 5.1 percent are considered.

like that in other urban areas of the North as well as the South, was highly unequal. The degree of inequality in Texas was slightly lower, probably because Texas towns were younger and smaller than those with which they were compared.

The final comparison is across time. How did wealthholding in antebellum Texas compare with that in the twentieth-century United States? Comprehensive data on the distribution of wealth in recent decades are difficult to obtain, mainly because no census since 1870 has required each individual to record the full value of his real and personal estate. Instead,

pp. 33-40) is supported by the findings of Stuart Blumin, "Mobility and Change in Ante-Bellum Philadelphia," in Stephan Thernstrom and Richard Sennett, eds., *Nineteenth-Century Cities: Essays in the New Urban History*, pp. 204-206.

studies of wealthholding in the twentieth century have had to rely upon indirect methods of estimating the distribution of wealth. Some researchers have determined *income* classes, for which there is ample information, and then converted them into *wealth* classes. Others have used federal estate tax returns, which they convert to estimates of wealthholding for the entire living population by the use of the "estate multiplier method." Still others employ survey research methods to compile sample studies of the total wealth held by "consumer spending units." Of course, the accuracy of estimates arrived at by these methods is open to question on several grounds. However, these measurements are the most comprehensive available, and their estimates probably do represent in a broad way the patterns of wealth distribution in the twentieth century.

Willford I. King's study of wealthholding in the United States at the close of 1921 provided the data we used to calculate a Gini index of .690.[10] This level of concentration, although somewhat lower than the .742 index for Texas in 1860, nevertheless represents a high degree of economic inequality. Moreover, King's estimates were for the distribution of wealth among all property owners rather than for all families whether they held property or not; therefore, his methodology (compared with ours) automatically created a downward bias in the degree of wealth concentration. If King's study had been based on the same system used in this book, the Gini index for 1921 would doubtless have risen to the .700's or perhaps higher. In any case, wealth in the United States in the early 1920's was about as unequally distributed as it was in Texas in 1860.

Robert J. Lampman's work on wealthholding in the United States from 1922 to 1956, employing the estate-multiplier method on estate tax returns for 1953, presented data that produced a Gini index of .636.[11]

[10]Willford I. King, "Wealth Distribution in the Continental United States at the Close of 1921," *Journal of the American Statistical Association* 22 (June, 1927), 150-152.

[11]Robert J. Lampman, *The Share of Top Wealth-holders in National Wealth, 1922-1956*, pp. 12-15, 213. For an international comparison, see Lampman's chart on page 212,

Again, the method of estimating wealth distribution here is different from ours. Nevertheless, the index of concentration for the United States in 1953 indicates that the nation continued to be characterized by considerable economic inequality.

Dorothy S. Projector and Gertrude S. Weiss's survey of consumer financial characteristics studied wealthholding among "consumer unit heads" (essentially the same unit used in our study) in the United States in 1962. They calculated a Gini coefficient of .760, very near the figure for Texas in 1860 (.742).[12] Thus, the study of twentieth-century wealthholding that in its unit of measurement most nearly approximated the approach used in our investigation (wealth distribution examined according to family units and adult individuals living alone) indicates that wealth was no more unequally distributed in slaveholding Texas than it is in the contemporary United States.

In summary, wealthholding in Texas appears to have been no more unequal than that in other areas of the United States before the Civil War, whether slave or free.[13] The picture of the antebellum United States as a land of relative economic equality is mythical. And the situation has not changed much in the more than one hundred years since the end of slavery. Indeed, the degree of wealth concentration for the United States in 1962 was quite comparable to that existing in the nation and Texas in 1860.

---

which indicates that wealth was more highly concentrated in England and Wales in 1946-1947 than in the United States in 1953.

[12]Dorothy S. Projector and Gertrude S. Weiss, eds., *Survey of Financial Characteristics of Consumers*, pp. 1-2, 30.

[13]We noted in chapter 3 possible objections to our method of determining the index of wealth concentration for Texas (and to comparisons based on this index). Discussion of why we considered wealthholding among the free population alone appears in appendix 2.

Chapter 9.

Summary and Conclusions

THERE was a high degree of inequality in the distribution of wealth among the entire free population of antebellum Texas. All important forms of wealth — real and personal property, slaves, and total wealth — were concentrated in the hands of a small group constituting less than 10 percent of all free Texans. Even when slaves are "freed" and considered as potential property owners rather than as property themselves, the level of concentration remains virtually the same (see appendix 2). The degree of economic inequality did not rise significantly between 1850 and 1860, but there was a noticeable increase in the percentage of individuals in the wealthiest group and in their share of property, indicating the increasingly dominant position of this minority. If the state is broken into four geographical areas differing in climate, soil, and extent of settlement, the most striking fact is that the high degree of concentration in wealthholding extended across all the regions of Texas with remarkable uniformity and stability from 1850 to 1860.

Turning from patterns of wealthholding to the characteristics of individual wealthholders, we see that the poorest class differed sharply from the other two classes, especially the wealthiest. Family heads in the lowest group owned on the average only 1/300 as much wealth as did family heads in the richest class. In addition, individuals in this poorest group were far more likely to be non-slaveowners, foreign-born, younger, and tradesmen or laborers. By contrast, heads of households in the richest class were vastly wealthier, virtually all owned slaves, 90 percent were native Southerners, a majority were forty-five years of age or older, and nearly all were engaged in farming, commerce, or the professions.

The agricultural population of antebellum Texas (roughly three-quarters of the total number of free families) was characterized statewide and in all four geographical regions by moderate to high degrees of inequality in the ownership of key forms of agricultural property and production. Cotton, the main cash crop, was far more highly concentrated than any other farm crop. As in the case of wealthholding in general, there was very little change in the level of concentration from 1850 to 1860. And also as in the case of wealthholding, the percentage of the richest class (large farmers) and their share of farm properties and products increased markedly during the decade.

Slaveholding farmers, who constituted about one-third of the agricultural population, controlled 60 to 70 percent of the improved acreage, cash value of farms, livestock value, and corn production, and approximately 90 percent of cotton production. There was some noticeable variation from region to region in the proportion of farmers who were slaveholders, but whatever their numbers, they held a disproportionately large share of farm property and production.

Wealthholding in Texas towns was more highly concentrated than in the state as a whole. Again, the degree of inequality changed only very slightly during the last antebellum decade. And wealth in these towns was generally controlled by a very small group of families dominated by the American-born, slaveholders, and merchants.

The political structure of antebellum Texas was democratic in that Texas had no property or tax-paying restrictions on voting or officeholding. On the other hand, the typical Texas political leader was generally much wealthier and usually held more slaves than the average Texan and was either a large farmer or a professional. Thus, the politics of antebellum Texas were a combination of democratic institutions and aristocratic leadership.

Before the Civil War wealth was no more unequally distributed in Texas than in other areas of the United States, whether slave or free. Furthermore, the situation has apparently not changed much in the years since 1860. In fact, the level of wealth concentration existing in Texas in 1860 was quite comparable to that for the United States in 1962.

Thus, the distribution of wealth and power in Texas was highly unequal in both 1850 and 1860. This conclusion suggests that Texas, and perhaps the slaveholding South in general, stood as an exception to the American egalitarian ideal. A comparison of circumstances in Texas with those in other areas of the United States in 1860 (and with those existing in the United States one hundred years later) strongly indicates, however, that a high level of concentration in economic and political power was not unique to Texas or the South. The egalitarian ideal was mythical in antebellum Texas, but was it not equally mythical elsewhere in the United States? An appreciation of the unequal distribution of wealth and power in Texas during the 1850's is essential to an understanding of economic and political developments in the antebellum period, but these circumstances should not be taken as distinctive or as not in keeping with the American experience.

Appendix 1.

Regional Tables: Wealthholding, 1850-1860

THE material in this appendix is described and analyzed in chapter 3, "Wealthholding in Texas, 1850-1860." As explained in that chapter, data on regional wealthholding are important, but the tables containing this information are too numerous to be included in the text. These tables are presented here for those who wish to make detailed comparisons.

TABLE 51

DISTRIBUTION OF REAL PROPERTY IN ANTEBELLUM TEXAS

REGION I (EAST TEXAS TIMBERLANDS), 1850 AND 1860

1850

$ Value of Real Property	0	1-249	250-499	500-999	1,000-4,999	5,000-9,999	10,000-19,999	20,000-49,999	50,000 and over	Totals
Percentage of Population	32.6	9.6	13.1	16.0	24.0	2.9	1.4	0.3	0.1	100.0
Percentage of Real Property	0.0	1.4	4.1	9.7	42.3	16.5	16.0	8.0	2.0	100.0

1860

Percentage of Population	28.8	4.2	9.6	14.2	32.3	6.3	3.3	1.1	0.2	100.0
Percentage of Real Property	0.0	0.3	1.5	4.3	29.4	18.1	19.1	13.5	13.8	100.0

TABLE 52

DISTRIBUTION OF REAL PROPERTY IN ANTEBELLUM TEXAS

REGION II (GULF COASTAL PLAINS), 1850 AND 1860

1850

$ Value of Real Property	0	1-249	250-499	500-999	1,000-4,999	5,000-9,999	10,000-19,999	20,000-49,999	50,000 and over	Totals
Percentage of Population	36.0	10.0	6.2	9.2	23.1	8.1	4.3	2.1	1.0	100.0
Percentage of Property	0.0	0.4	0.7	1.9	15.3	17.8	18.3	17.9	27.7	100.0

1860

Percentage of Population	33.6	2.7	5.6	9.2	25.9	6.3	7.4	5.1	4.2	100.0
Percentage of Property	0.0	0.1	0.3	0.8	8.2	5.8	13.9	22.8	48.1	100.0

TABLE 53

DISTRIBUTION OF REAL PROPERTY IN ANTEBELLUM TEXAS

REGION III (NORTH-CENTRAL PRAIRIE), 1850 AND 1860

1850

$ Value of Real Property	0	1-249	250-499	500-999	1,000-4,999	5,000-9,999	10,000-19,999	20,000-49,999	50,000 and over	Totals
Percentage of Population	35.6	10.7	14.4	17.8	17.1	2.9	1.3	0.2	0.0	100.0
Percentage of Real Property	0.0	1.8	5.3	12.7	33.6	20.2	18.2	8.2	0.0	100.0

1860

Percentage of Population	36.5	4.5	8.4	13.7	28.6	4.2	2.7	1.0	0.4	100.0
Percentage of Real Property	0.0	0.3	1.6	5.0	31.5	14.1	16.3	14.3	16.9	100.0

TABLE 54

DISTRIBUTION OF REAL PROPERTY IN ANTEBELLUM TEXAS

REGION IV (SOUTH-CENTRAL AREA), 1850 AND 1860

1850

$ Value of Real Property	0	1-249	250-499	500-999	1,000-4,999	5,000-9,999	10,000-19,999	20,000-49,999	50,000 and over	Totals
Percentage of Population	36.7	13.8	8.6	9.7	21.9	5.0	3.0	0.8	0.5	100.0
Percentage of Real Property	0.0	1.2	1.7	3.4	25.1	17.9	21.0	13.0	16.7	100.0

1860

$ Value of Real Property	0	1-249	250-499	500-999	1,000-4,999	5,000-9,999	10,000-19,999	20,000-49,999	50,000 and over	Totals
Percentage of Population	35.7	4.4	7.8	11.1	28.1	4.9	4.3	3.0	0.7	100.0
Percentage of Real Property	0.0	0.2	0.9	2.5	20.5	10.6	20.0	30.8	14.5	100.0

TABLE 55

DISTRIBUTION OF SLAVE PROPERTY IN ANTEBELLUM TEXAS

REGION I (EAST TEXAS TIMBERLANDS), 1850 AND 1860

1850

Number of Slaves	0	1-4	5-9	10-19	20-29	30-39	40-49	50-99	100+	Totals
Percentage of Population	64.4	19.2	8.4	5.6	1.5	0.4	0.3	0.2	0.0	100.0
Percentage of Slave Property	0.0	16.5	22.9	30.9	14.3	5.3	4.7	5.3	0.0	100.0

1860

Number of Slaves	0	1-4	5-9	10-19	20-29	30-39	40-49	50-99	100+	Totals
Percentage of Population	65.7	15.6	7.8	6.8	2.1	0.7	0.7	0.6	0.1	100.0
Percentage of Slave Property	0.0	10.3	16.2	27.2	14.5	6.5	9.6	11.9	3.8	100.0

TABLE 56

DISTRIBUTION OF SLAVE PROPERTY IN ANTEBELLUM TEXAS

REGION II (GULF COASTAL PLAINS), 1850 AND 1860

1850

Number of Slaves	0	1-4	5-9	10-19	20-29	30-39	40-49	50-99	100+	Totals
Percentage of Population	67.1	16.2	8.1	4.1	1.6	0.9	0.7	1.2	0.1	100.0
Percentage of Slave Property	0.0	9.3	14.4	15.8	11.3	8.2	9.2	22.2	9.6	100.0

1860

Percentage of Population	71.4	11.2	7.1	5.6	1.3	1.6	0.0	1.1	0.7	100.0
Percentage of Slave Property	0.0	6.7	11.5	19.5	8.0	12.9	0.0	17.3	24.1	100.0

TABLE 57

DISTRIBUTION OF SLAVE PROPERTY IN ANTEBELLUM TEXAS

REGION III (NORTH-CENTRAL PRAIRIE), 1850 AND 1860

1850

Number of Slaves	0	1-4	5-9	10-19	20-29	30-39	40-49	50-99	100+	Totals
Percentage of Population	82.3	12.8	2.8	1.6	0.1	0.3	0.1	0.0	0.0	100.0
Percentage of Slave Property	0.0	31.3	22.7	26.1	3.7	9.8	6.4	0.0	0.0	100.0

1860

Percentage of Population	80.1	11.6	5.4	2.1	0.5	0.1	0.1	0.1	0.0	100.0
Percentage of Slave Property	0.0	21.9	30.5	25.9	10.8	4.5	2.6	3.8	0.0	100.0

TABLE 58

DISTRIBUTION OF SLAVE PROPERTY IN ANTEBELLUM TEXAS

REGION IV (SOUTH-CENTRAL AREA), 1850 AND 1860

1850

Number of Slaves	0	1-4	5-9	10-19	20-29	30-39	40-49	50-99	100+	Totals
Percentage of Population	73.6	13.6	7.7	3.4	1.2	0.4	0.1	0.0	0.0	100.0
Percentage of Slave Property	0.0	16.7	31.4	26.1	16.6	7.0	2.2	0.0	0.0	100.0

1860

Percentage of Population	75.9	11.2	5.3	4.4	1.5	1.2	0.3	0.2	0.0	100.0
Percentage of Slave Property	0.0	11.1	15.2	26.6	15.9	17.2	6.8	7.2	0.0	100.0

TABLE 59

DISTRIBUTION OF PERSONAL PROPERTY IN ANTEBELLUM TEXAS

REGION I (EAST TEXAS TIMBERLANDS), 1860

$ Value of Personal Property	0	1-249	250-499	500-999	1,000-4,999	5,000-9,999	10,000-19,999	20,000-49,999	50,000 & over	Totals
Percentage of Population	4.7	14.4	16.5	18.1	24.8	9.6	7.4	3.5	1.0	100.0
Percentage of Personal Property	0.0	0.5	1.3	2.7	13.3	15.5	22.9	24.4	19.4	100.0

TABLE 60

DISTRIBUTION OF PERSONAL PROPERTY IN ANTEBELLUM TEXAS

REGION II (GULF COASTAL PLAINS), 1860

$ Value of Personal Property	0	1-249	250-499	500-999	1,000-4,999	5,000-9,999	10,000-19,999	20,000-49,999	50,000 & over	Totals
Percentage of Population	28.2	12.5	8.3	6.5	20.8	8.2	5.8	7.2	2.0	100.0
Percentage of Personal Property	0.0	0.3	0.4	0.7	6.7	9.2	13.1	37.3	32.3	100.0

TABLE 61

DISTRIBUTION OF PERSONAL PROPERTY IN ANTEBELLUM TEXAS

REGION III (NORTH-CENTRAL PRAIRIE), 1860

$ Value of Personal Property	0	1-249	250-499	500-999	1,000-4,999	5,000-9,999	10,000-19,999	20,000-49,999	50,000 & over	Totals
Percentage of Population	4.7	12.1	17.3	19.6	35.0	7.1	2.8	1.3	0.1	100.0
Percentage of Personal Property	0.0	0.8	2.7	5.8	32.5	22.0	17.1	17.1	2.0	100.0

TABLE 62

DISTRIBUTION OF PERSONAL PROPERTY IN ANTEBELLUM TEXAS

REGION IV (SOUTH-CENTRAL AREA), 1860

$ Value of Personal Property	0	1-249	250-499	500-999	1,000-4,999	5,000-9,999	10,000-19,999	20,000-49,999	50,000 & over	Totals
Percentage of Population	16.3	14.0	12.5	16.2	22.0	9.0	5.4	3.9	0.7	100.0
Percentage of Personal Property	0.0	0.5	1.2	2.9	13.7	16.0	20.4	29.7	15.6	100.0

TABLE 63

DISTRIBUTION OF WEALTH IN ANTEBELLUM TEXAS

REGION I (EAST TEXAS TIMBERLANDS), 1860

$ Value of Wealth	0	1-249	250-499	500-999	1,000-4,999	5,000-9,999	10,000-19,999	20,000-49,999	50,000 & over	Totals
Percentage of Population	3.8	10.1	9.1	13.6	34.7	12.0	9.3	5.6	1.8	100.0
Percentage of Wealth	0.0	0.2	0.5	1.5	11.9	12.7	20.4	26.4	26.4	100.0

TABLE 64

DISTRIBUTION OF WEALTH IN ANTEBELLUM TEXAS

REGION II (GULF COASTAL PLAINS), 1860

$ Value of Wealth	0	1-249	250-499	500-999	1,000-4,999	5,000-9,999	10,000-19,999	20,000-49,999	50,000 & over	Totals
Percentage of Population	18.8	3.8	5.8	10.5	29.1	8.5	8.5	7.2	7.8	100.0
Percentage of Wealth	0.0	0.1	0.1	0.6	4.9	4.7	9.2	18.9	61.5	100.0

TABLE 65

DISTRIBUTION OF WEALTH IN ANTEBELLUM TEXAS

REGION III (NORTH-CENTRAL PRAIRIE), 1860

$ Value of Wealth	0	1-249	250-499	500-999	1,000-4,999	5,000-9,999	10,000-19,999	20,000-49,999	50,000 & over	Totals
Percentage of Population	4.5	8.4	10.0	16.4	40.2	11.3	6.1	2.3	0.8	100.0
Percentage of Wealth	0.0	0.3	0.8	2.7	22.8	19.3	20.6	16.8	16.7	100.0

TABLE 66

DISTRIBUTION OF WEALTH IN ANTEBELLUM TEXAS

REGION IV (SOUTH-CENTRAL AREA), 1860

$ Value of Wealth	0	1-249	250 499	500-999	1,000-4,999	5,000-9,999	10,000-19,999	20,000-49,999	50,000 & over	Totals
Percentage of Population	14.5	8.0	7.0	11.8	32.1	11.1	7.1	5.9	2.5	100.0
Percentage of Wealth	0.0	0.2	0.4	1.2	11.5	11.6	15.5	28.2	31.4	100.0

Appendix 2.

Slave Property and the Distribution of Wealth in Texas, 1860

AS noted in chapters 3 and 8, one objection to our method of determining wealth concentration for antebellum Texas might be that we consider wealth distributions among the free population alone rather than among the entire population, both slave and free. We believe this possible objection to be somewhat ahistorical since, questions of morality aside, slaves were property and not property owners. The only actual historical wealth distribution for Texas in 1860 is that for the free population (see table 67). The question, however, remains — how would wealth have been distributed *if* the slave population had been free (and therefore potential property holders)?[1] The answer to this question is interesting in itself, and, furthermore, it will demonstrate whether or not the counting of slaves as potential property owners rather than as property has any noticeable effect on the level of wealth concentration in antebellum Texas.

Obviously, this question can be answered only through a counterfactual approach, that is, by considering what "might have been," given

[1]Robert E. Gallman ("Trends in the Size Distribution of Wealth in the Nineteenth Century: Some Speculations," in Lee Soltow, ed., *Six Papers on the Size Distribution of Wealth and Income*, pp. 6-9, 15) examined this historical question and emphasized its importance. Robert W. Fogel and Stanley L. Engerman (*Time on the Cross: The Economics of Negro Slavery*, II, 165) touch on the wealth distribution question and say that "what remains to be done is to construct the wealth distribution of the entire population, slave as well as free." Gavin Wright (" 'Economic Democracy' and the Concentration of Agricultural Wealth in the Cotton South, 1850-1860," *Agricultural History* 44 [January, 1970], 69) introduces a different perspective on this issue by stressing the "ethically objectionable" aspect of considering slaves only as property and not as human beings.

certain circumstances other than what actually was. Counterfactualization does not produce history in the traditional sense, but this particular historical issue cannot be dealt with in any other manner.

The actual wealth distribution for Texas in 1860 is demonstrated in table 67, a repetition of table 11 in chapter 3. As previously stated, this table displays an unequal distribution in favor of a small minority. The Gini index calculated from the figures of this table is .742.

Of the wealthholders represented in table 67, 27.3 percent were slaveowners, and they owned 12,575 slaves in holdings ranging from a single bondsman to plantation forces of more than 100 slaves.[2] In order to "free" the slaves so that they could be considered as potential property holders, we excluded the value of all bondsmen from our calculations. This was accomplished not by formula, but by reducing the total wealth of each slaveowner by the value of his slave property. The number of slaves in each holding was multiplied by $850, the average value of slaves in Texas in 1860, and the product was subtracted from that individual's wealth.[3] This step produced a new distribution, represented in table 68.

It would be ideal to know the age, sex, and condition, and therefore value, of each slave involved in our sample, but this is plainly impossible. Furthermore, the use of an average value per slave may be defended on the grounds that the Texas slave population was normally distributed in terms of age and sex characteristics (i.e., there was no particular concentration of males or of any special age groups among Texas slaves). Thus, an average value is appropriate for an "average" slave population. A test of the validity of the $850 figure is to determine whether or not large

[2]The absolute number of slaves used here is based on our sample rather than on the entire population.

[3]The estimate of $850 per slave was derived from Ulrich B. Phillips, *American Negro Slavery: A Survey of the Supply, Employment, and Control of Negro Labor as Determined by the Plantation Regime*, pp. 368-370; Robert Evans, Jr., "The Economics of American Negro Slavery, 1830-1860," in *Aspects of Labor Economics: A Conference of the Universities-National Bureau Committee for Economic Research*, pp. 199-202; and Randolph Campbell, "Local Archives as a Source of Slave Prices: Harrison County, Texas, as a Test Case," *The Historian* 36 (August, 1974), 660-670.

TABLE 67

DISTRIBUTION OF WEALTH IN TEXAS, 1860

(Slave Property Included)

$ Value of Wealth	0	1-249	250-499	500-999	1,000-4,999	5,000-9,999	10,000-19,999	20,000-49,999	50,000 & over	Totals
Percentage of Family Heads	8.0	8.5	8.6	13.7	35.1	11.2	7.8	4.9	2.2	100.0
Percentage of Wealth	0.0	0.2	0.5	1.5	12.5	12.2	17.2	23.8	32.2	100.0

Gini Index = .742

TABLE 68

DISTRIBUTION OF WEALTH IN TEXAS, 1860

(Slave Property Excluded)

$ Value of Wealth	0	1-249	250-499	500-999	1,000-4,999	5,000-9,999	10,000-19,999	20,000-49,999	50,000 & over	Totals
Percentage of Family Heads	10.0	8.9	9.0	14.8	39.4	9.3	4.8	2.7	1.1	100.0
Percentage of Wealth	0.0	0.3	0.7	2.4	21.1	15.1	15.6	19.4	25.4	100.0

Gini Index = .754

amounts of personal property remained in the hands of wealthy slaveholders after the subtraction of wealth in slaves. If large amounts did remain, this could indicate that the $850 figure was not high enough to eliminate all or most of the slaves' value. There were 189 slaveholders in our sample who owned personal property valued at $20,000 or more in 1860. Once slave values (at $850 per slave) were subtracted from the personal property of each individual, only 38 of these wealthy slaveholders remained, and 10 of the 38 were non-farmers (merchants, for example) who probably held most of their personal property in forms other than slaves. Therefore, the $850 figure does seem to represent the average value of Texas slaves in 1860.

Incidentally, the exclusion of slave property from our calculations did not dramatically alter the level of wealth concentration among the free population. This rather unexpected result is not difficult to explain. Once slave property was excluded, there was a reduction in the percentage of individuals in the richest classes ($20,000 and over), but the proprotion of wealth those individuals owned did not decline as much, making those rich individuals who remained *relatively* richer. In addition, once slave property was omitted, there were somewhat higher percentages of family heads in both the zero wealthholder and other lower wealth classes. Both these situations tend to *raise* the level of concentration very slightly rather than lower it. Moreover, the removal of slave property affects personal property only, leaving the notably unequal distribution of real estate intact (see table 8 in chapter 3). Thus, even when slave property is omitted from consideration, the degree of concentration in all other forms of wealth in antebellum Texas remains virtually the same, moving only from .742 to .754.

This exclusion of slave values from the wealth distribution for 1860 does not take into consideration the 12,575 slaves who were owned by the free families in our sample. If not enslaved, these black Southerners would have been potential property holders. Since our basic data unit was the family, we converted the 12,575 slaves into 2,286 families, using the average family size among white Texans in 1860 (5.5 persons per family) as a divisor.[4] The next step was to decide how much wealth to assign to each of our 2,286 "freed" black families. One approach was to assume (hypothetically) that all these "freed" families were zero wealthholders,

[4]The average size of Texas families was calculated from the figures in *Eighth Census of the United States, 1860, Mortality and Miscellaneous Statistics*, p. 349. The age and sex distributions of Texas slaves were very similar to those for Texas whites. Therefore, it is appropriate to assume that the average "freed" family size would be comparable to that of free whites.

who owned no real or personal property at all. The results of this approach are presented in table 69. When compared with the results presented in table 67, the counting of "freed" blacks as zero wealthholders greatly increased the percentage of Texas families with no wealth and resulted in a higher Gini index of concentration (.812).

It is unrealistic, however, to assume that not a single one of these black potential wealthholders would have owned real or personal property. It does not necessarily follow that propertyless slaves would have remained propertyless as freedmen.[5] A more realistic approach, one based on the best data available, is to assign to these "freed" families wealthholdings comparable to those of the free Negro families who actually lived in Texas in 1860. There were 355 free Negroes in the state in 1860. We recorded the wealthholdings of all those in counties having five or more free Negroes (i.e., those counties containing enough free Negroes to constitute an average-sized Texas family) and then determined a wealth distribution for those families.[6] The final step was to construct a new wealth distribution for the state (table 70) that counts "freed" black families as wealthholders comparable to actual free Negro families in Texas in 1860 and adds them to the free population with slave property excluded from consideration. In short, we hypothetically "emancipated" the slaves and merged them into the general population.

This was done by determining the percentage of free Negro families that fell into each interval of our basic wealth distribution table and then

[5]This approach was employed for the whole South by Gallman, "Size Distribution of Wealth in the Nineteenth Century," pp. 6-9, 15. Lee Soltow, in commenting on Gallman's paper, specifically criticized the assumption that all "freed" black families would have been propertyless (*ibid.*, pp. 25-26).

[6]The number of free Negroes and their counties of residence were determined from *Eighth Census of the United States, 1860, Population*, pp. 484-486. Some of those persons listed under the heading "Free Colored" were in fact Indians or Mexicans; we excluded these non-Negroes from our calculations. Ironically, Schedule IV (Slave Inhabitants) revealed that four of the free Negro families owned slave property. We subtracted the value of their slaves from their wealthholdings in order to construct the necessary wealth distribution in table 70.

TABLE 69

DISTRIBUTION OF WEALTH IN TEXAS, 1860

(Counting "Freed" Blacks as Zero Wealthholders)

$ Value of Wealth	0	1-249	250-499	500-999	1,000-4,999	5,000-9,999	10,000-19,999	20,000-49,999	50,000 & over	Totals
Percentage of Family Heads	38.5	6.5	6.2	10.1	26.9	6.4	3.3	1.8	0.8	100.0
Percentage of Wealth	0.0	0.3	0.7	2.4	21.1	15.1	15.6	19.4	25.4	100.0

Gini Index = .812

TABLE 70

DISTRIBUTION OF WEALTH IN TEXAS, 1860

(Counting "Freed" Blacks as Wealthholders Comparable to Free Negroes, 1860)

$ Value of Wealth	0	1-249	250-499	500-999	1,000-4,999	5,000-9,999	10,000-19,999	20,000-49,999	50,000 & over	Totals
Percentage of Family Heads	21.7	8.0	9.2	12.1	33.9	8.3	4.2	1.8	0.8	100.0
Percentage of Wealth	0.0	0.3	0.9	2.4	23.1	17.4	17.6	16.6	21.7	100.0

Gini Index = .757

multiplying that percentage by the total number of "freed" black families to be entered into the new wealth distribution. For example, 46.9 percent of the free Negro families were zero wealthholders; therefore, we added 46.9 percent of the 2,286 "freed" families (1,073) to the number of families in the zero interval of the new wealth distribution. The next 6.2 percent of the free Negro families fell in the $1-249 interval, so 6.2 percent of the 2,286 "freed" families (142) were added to the $1-249 interval. This process continued through the $10,000-19,999 interval, the highest into which any of the free Negro families fell.

In order to determine the amount of wealth the "freed" families to be added in each interval would have owned, we took the mean wealth of the free Negro families in each interval and multiplied that figure by the number of "freed" families being added to that interval. For example, the free Negro families in the $1-249 interval owned an average of $75 in property value. We multiplied $75 by the 142 "freed" families being added to that interval and arrived at a total of $10,650, which was then added to the wealth in the $1-249 interval of the new distribution. This process continued through all the intervals into which any of the free Negro families fell. In short, we assigned to the "freed" blacks in each interval wealthholdings of the same average size as those owned by free Negroes in those intervals. The absolute numbers of families and wealth values in the new wealth distribution were then converted to percentages, and the result was table 70.

Compared with the actual situation in 1860 (table 67), the most realistic counterfactual wealth distribution reveals a higher percentage of zero wealthholders but a smaller proportion of individuals in the richest classes ($20,000 or more in wealth). This new hypothetical distribution produces a Gini index (.757) nearly identical to that drawn from the actual situation in 1860 (.742). It may seem surprising that the deduction of an asset held primarily by the wealthier classes did not reduce the degree of wealth concentration. The lack of change is explained, however, by three circumstances. First, there is a noticeable increase in the percentage of zero wealthholders, a development that should have increased the degree of concentration; second, there is a noticeable increase in the proportion of property held by the middle class (for example, the percentage of all wealth held by those owning between $1,000 and $4,999 increased from 12.5 to 23.1 percent, whereas the percentage of the total population in that group actually declined slightly), a development that should have reduced the degree of inequality; and third, the percentage of people in the richest class declined more rapidly than did their share of total wealth, a development that should have increased the degree of inequality. Thus, these various developments balance each other out, producing a level of concentration virtually identical to that actually existing in 1860. Therefore, the procedure of "freeing" the slaves and considering them as families with property holdings comparable to those of free Negroes does not produce a more equal or unequal wealthholding situation in antebellum Texas.[7]

We thus conclude that (1) the method used in this study to determine the degree of wealth concentration for Texas in 1860 is both historically realistic and accurately indicative of wealthholding in general. Indices of wealth concentration were nearly identical whether slaves were treated as property or "freed" and treated as potential property holders. (2) The exclusion of slaves from consideration, either as property or as potential property owners, contrary to what might be expected, did not significantly alter the degree of inequality in wealthholding. Indeed, the Gini index for free families is minutely higher (.754) when slave property is excluded from the calculations.

[7]It must be remembered that at every stage of this counterfactual approach the impact of the slave system on wealth distributions extends beyond the value of slave property. For example, it seems certain that the ownership of large slave forces was closely related to the ownership of large amounts of property in other forms (e.g., improved acreage). Therefore, the subtraction of slave values does not totally eliminate the impact of the slave system on wealth distributions. Nevertheless, wealth in slaves is obviously the major element in this type of calculation, and it is startling to discover that its removal has so little effect on the overall distribution of wealth.

Appendix 3.

Regional Tables: Agricultural Property and Production, 1850-1860

THE material in this appendix is described and analyzed in chapter 5, "Distribution of Agricultural Property and Production, 1850-1860," As explained in that chapter, data on regional distributions of farm property and production are important, but the tables are too numerous to be included in the text. These tables are presented here for those who wish to make detailed comparisons.

TABLE 71

DISTRIBUTION OF IMPROVED ACREAGE IN ANTEBELLUM TEXAS
REGION I (EAST TEXAS TIMBERLANDS), 1850 AND 1860

1850

No. of Improved Acres	0	1-49	50-99	100-199	200-299	300-399	400-499	500-999	1,000+	Totals
% of Farm Population	28.8	48.5	14.1	6.0	1.4	0.8	0.1	0.2	0.1	100.0
% of Improved Acres	0.0	31.6	24.9	21.2	8.3	7.4	1.1	4.0	1.5	100.0
% of Slaveholding Farmers	5.6	13.0	9.8	5.8	1.4	0.8	0.1	0.2	0.1	36.8
% of Improved Acres	0.0	10.2	17.6	20.3	8.3	7.4	1.1	4.0	1.5	70.4
% of Non-Slaveholding Farmers	23.2	35.5	4.3	0.2	0.0	0.0	0.0	0.0	0.0	63.2
% of Improved Acres	0.0	21.4	7.3	0.9	0.0	0.0	0.0	0.0	0.0	29.6

1860

No. of Improved Acres	0	1-49	50-99	100-199	200-299	300-399	400-499	500-999	1,000+	Totals
% of Farm Population	17.1	45.0	19.3	11.8	3.1	1.4	1.0	1.2	0.1	100.0
% of Improved Acres	0.0	18.2	19.9	23.9	11.2	7.1	6.6	12.0	1.1	100.0
% of Slaveholding Farmers	1.9	7.7	11.1	10.6	3.1	1.4	1.0	1.2	0.1	38.1
% of Improved Acres	0.0	3.6	12.0	21.7	11.2	7.1	6.6	12.0	1.1	75.3
% of Non-Slaveholding Farmers	15.2	37.3	8.2	1.2	0.0	0.0	0.0	0.0	0.0	61.9
% of Improved Acres	0.0	14.6	7.9	2.2	0.0	0.0	0.0	0.0	0.0	24.7

TABLE 72

DISTRIBUTION OF IMPROVED ACREAGE IN ANTEBELLUM TEXAS
REGION II (GULF COASTAL PLAINS), 1850 AND 1860

1850

No. of Improved Acres	0	1-49	50-99	100-199	200-299	300-399	400-499	500-999	1000+	Totals
% of Farm Population	27.9	51.8	8.2	5.6	3.8	0.6	0.3	1.5	0.3	100.0
% of Improved Acres	0.0	20.0	11.3	16.1	18.9	4.7	2.6	18.9	7.5	100.0
% of Slaveholding Farmers	5.6	21.2	7.3	5.6	3.8	0.6	0.3	1.5	0.3	46.2
% of Improved Acres	0.0	10.3	10.1	16.1	18.9	4.7	2.6	18.9	7.5	89.1
% of Non-Slaveholding Farmers	22.3	30.6	0.9	0.0	0.0	0.0	0.0	0.0	0.0	53.8
% of Improved Acres	0.0	9.7	1.2	0.0	0.0	0.0	0.0	0.0	0.0	10.9

1860

% of Farm Population	11.4	47.7	13.4	10.7	5.4	2.7	2.0	6.0	0.7	100.0
% of Improved Acres	0.0	7.8	8.1	12.8	10.6	8.1	7.2	36.7	8.7	100.0
% of Slaveholding Farmers	3.4	14.8	10.1	10.7	5.4	2.7	2.0	6.0	0.7	55.8
% of Improved Acres	0.0	3.1	6.2	12.8	10.6	8.1	7.2	36.7	8.7	93.4
% of Non-Slaveholding Farmers	8.0	32.9	3.3	0.0	0.0	0.0	0.0	0.0	0.0	44.2
% of Improved Acres	0.0	4.7	1.9	0.0	0.0	0.0	0.0	0.0	0.0	6.6

TABLE 73

DISTRIBUTION OF IMPROVED ACREAGE IN ANTEBELLUM TEXAS
REGION III (NORTH-CENTRAL PRAIRIE), 1850 AND 1860

1850

No. of Improved Acres	0	1-49	50-99	100-199	200-299	300-399	400-499	500-999	1000+	Totals
% of Farm Population	20.5	67.6	8.5	2.9	0.4	0.0	0.0	0.1	0.0	100.0
% of Improved Acres	0.0	55.2	22.8	14.8	3.3	0.0	0.0	3.9	0.0	100.0
% of Slaveholding Farmers	1.3	10.6	4.0	2.0	0.4	0.0	0.0	0.1	0.0	18.4
% of Improved Acres	0.0	10.4	11.1	10.1	3.3	0.0	0.0	3.9	0.0	38.8
% of Non-Slaveholding Farmers	19.2	57.0	4.5	0.9	0.0	0.0	0.0	0.0	0.0	81.6
% of Improved Acres	0.0	44.8	11.7	4.7	0.0	0.0	0.0	0.0	0.0	61.2

1860

No. of Improved Acres	0	1-49	50-99	100-199	200-299	300-399	400-499	500-999	1000+	Totals
% of Farm Population	33.6	43.6	13.7	6.4	1.5	0.5	0.4	0.3	0.0	100.0
% of Improved Acres	0.0	29.8	25.9	22.0	9.4	3.9	4.2	4.8	0.0	100.0
% of Slaveholding Farmers	2.8	7.1	6.1	4.1	1.3	0.3	0.3	0.2	0.0	22.2
% of Improved Acres	0.0	6.1	12.0	14.2	8.3	2.4	3.0	3.3	0.0	49.3
% of Non-Slaveholding Farmers	30.8	36.5	7.6	2.3	0.2	0.2	0.1	0.1	0.0	77.8
% of Improved Acres	0.0	23.7	13.9	7.8	1.1	1.5	1.2	1.5	0.0	50.7

TABLE 74

DISTRIBUTION OF IMPROVED ACREAGE IN ANTEBELLUM TEXAS
REGION IV (SOUTH-CENTRAL AREA), 1850 AND 1860

1850

No. of Improved Acres	0	1-49	50-99	100-199	200-299	300-399	400-499	500-999	1000+	Totals
% of Farm Population	23.8	55.5	12.5	5.9	1.5	0.2	0.2	0.3	0.1	100.0
% of Improved Acres	0.0	31.5	24.0	22.4	9.5	1.6	1.8	4.8	4.4	100.0
% of Slaveholding Farmers	2.4	14.7	9.5	5.5	1.2	0.2	0.2	0.3	0.1	34.1
% of Improved Acres	0.0	11.1	18.6	20.6	7.5	1.6	1.8	4.8	4.4	70.4
% of Non-Slaveholding Farmers	21.4	40.8	3.0	0.4	0.3	0.0	0.0	0.0	0.0	65.9
% of Improved Acres	0.0	20.4	5.4	1.8	2.0	0.0	0.0	0.0	0.0	29.6

1860

No. of Improved Acres	0	1-49	50-99	100-199	200-299	300-399	400-499	500-999	1000+	Totals
% of Farm Population	22.8	48.6	13.5	7.3	3.9	2.2	0.8	0.5	0.4	100.0
% of Improved Acres	0.0	19.0	16.1	17.0	15.5	13.2	6.4	6.1	6.7	100.0
% of Slaveholding Farmers	2.7	7.7	7.3	6.4	3.2	2.2	0.8	0.5	0.4	31.2
% of Improved Acres	0.0	3.7	9.1	15.0	12.5	13.2	6.4	6.1	6.7	72.7
% of Non-Slaveholding Farmers	20.1	40.9	6.2	0.9	0.7	0.0	0.0	0.0	0.0	68.8
% of Improved Acres	0.0	15.3	7.0	2.0	3.0	0.0	0.0	0.0	0.0	27.3

TABLE 75

DISTRIBUTION OF CASH VALUE OF FARM IN ANTEBELLUM TEXAS
REGION I (EAST TEXAS TIMBERLANDS), 1850 AND 1860

1850

$ of Cash Value	0	1-249	250-499	500-999	1,000-4,999	5,000-9,999	10,000-19,999	20,000-49,999	50,000+	Totals
% of Farm Population	30.0	12.4	14.5	17.4	23.3	1.9	0.4	0.1	0.0	100.0
% of Cash Value	0.0	2.4	6.2	14.4	54.3	14.1	5.8	2.8	0.0	100.0
% of Slaveholding Farmers	5.9	2.4	4.0	6.9	15.4	1.6	0.4	0.1	0.0	36.6
% of Cash Value	0.0	0.5	1.7	5.8	37.7	12.0	5.8	2.8	0.0	66.3
% of Non-Slaveholding Farmers	24.1	10.0	10.5	10.5	7.9	0.3	0.0	0.0	0.0	63.3
% of Cash Value	0.0	1.9	4.5	8.6	16.6	2.1	0.0	0.0	0.0	33.7

1860

$ of Cash Value	0	1-249	250-499	500-999	1,000-4,999	5,000-9,999	10,000-19,999	20,000-49,999	50,000+	Totals
% of Farm Population	17.5	7.3	11.5	17.5	38.0	5.3	2.4	0.5	0.0	100.0
% of Cash Value	0.0	0.6	2.3	6.7	45.4	19.2	16.9	8.9	0.0	100.0
% of Slaveholding Farmers	2.1	0.9	1.9	3.6	21.9	5.0	2.2	0.5	0.0	38.1
% of Cash Value	0.0	0.1	0.4	1.5	29.3	18.1	15.5	8.9	0.0	73.8
% of Non-slaveholding Farmers	15.4	6.4	9.6	13.9	16.1	0.3	0.2	0.0	0.0	61.9
% of Cash Value	0.0	0.5	1.9	5.2	16.1	1.1	1.4	0.0	0.0	26.2

TABLE 76

DISTRIBUTION OF CASH VALUE OF FARM IN ANTEBELLUM TEXAS
REGION II (GULF COASTAL PLAINS), 1850 AND 1860

1850

$ of Cash Value	0	1-249	250-499	500-999	1,000-4,999	5,000-9,999	10,000-19,999	20,000-49,999	50,000+	Totals
% of Farm Population	26.8	16.5	7.9	10.0	26.8	7.9	2.6	1.5	0.0	100.0
% of Cash Value	0.0	1.0	1.4	3.5	29.4	27.5	17.3	19.9	0.0	100.0
% of Slaveholding Farmers	5.0	2.7	3.2	6.2	18.2	7.1	2.4	1.5	0.0	46.3
% of Cash Value	0.0	0.2	0.6	2.3	22.7	24.3	15.3	19.9	0.0	85.3
% of Non-Slaveholding Farmers	21.8	13.8	4.7	3.8	8.6	0.8	0.2	0.0	0.0	53.7
% of Cash Value	0.0	0.8	0.8	1.2	6.7	3.2	2.0	0.0	0.0	14.7

1860

% of Farm Population	11.4	5.4	9.4	11.4	30.2	9.4	8.7	8.1	6.0	100.0
% of Cash Value	0.0	0.1	0.4	0.8	7.9	6.2	11.3	27.6	45.7	100.0
% of Slaveholding Farmers	3.4	1.4	2.0	1.3	18.1	8.1	8.0	7.4	6.0	55.7
% of Cash Value	0.0	0.1	0.1	0.1	5.5	5.3	10.6	25.9	45.7	93.3
% of Non-Slaveholding Farmers	8.0	4.0	7.4	10.1	12.1	1.3	0.7	0.7	0.0	44.3
% of Cash Value	0.0	0.0	0.3	0.7	2.4	0.9	0.7	1.7	0.0	6.7

TABLE 77

DISTRIBUTION OF CASH VALUE OF FARM IN ANTEBELLUM TEXAS
REGION III (NORTH-CENTRAL PRAIRIE), 1850 AND 1860

1850

$ of Cash Value	0	1-249	250-499	500-999	1,000-4,999	5,000-9,999	10,000-19,999	20,000-49,999	50,000+	Totals
% of Farm Population	20.3	21.6	19.2	21.3	16.0	1.3	0.3	0.0	0.0	100.0
% of Cash Value	0.0	4.4	10.1	21.0	42.4	14.5	7.6	0.0	0.0	100.0
% of Slaveholding Farmers	1.3	2.1	3.1	4.4	6.7	0.5	0.3	0.0	0.0	18.4
% of Cash Value	0.0	0.5	1.7	4.0	19.5	6.0	7.6	0.0	0.0	39.3
% of Non-Slaveholding Farmers	19.0	19.5	16.1	16.9	9.3	0.8	0.0	0.0	0.0	81.6
% of Cash Value	0.0	3.9	8.4	17.0	22.9	8.5	0.0	0.0	0.0	60.7

1860

$ of Cash Value	0	1-249	250-499	500-999	1,000-4,999	5,000-9,999	10,000-19,999	20,000-49,999	50,000+	Totals
% of Farm Population	33.5	5.2	8.6	15.3	30.2	3.8	2.2	0.9	0.3	100.0
% of Cash Value	0.0	0.5	1.8	6.1	36.1	14.2	15.0	13.1	13.2	100.0
% of Slaveholding Farmers	3.1	0.4	1.0	1.5	10.7	2.9	1.7	0.7	0.3	22.3
% of Cash Value	0.0	0.1	0.2	0.6	14.0	10.9	11.4	10.8	13.2	61.2
% of Non-Slaveholding Farmers	30.4	4.8	7.6	13.8	19.5	0.9	0.5	0.2	0.0	77.7
% of Cash Value	0.0	0.4	1.6	5.5	22.1	3.3	3.6	2.3	0.0	38.8

TABLE 78

DISTRIBUTION OF CASH VALUE OF FARM IN ANTEBELLUM TEXAS
REGION IV (SOUTH-CENTRAL AREA), 1850 AND 1860

1850

$ of Cash Value	0	1-249	250-499	500-999	1,000-4,999	5,000-9,999	10,000-19,999	20,000-49,999	50,000+	Totals
% of Farm Population	24.4	13.4	12.8	19.5	25.7	2.8	0.9	0.3	0.2	100.0
% of Cash Value	0.0	1.7	3.8	10.8	43.9	14.8	10.1	5.6	9.3	100.0
% of Slaveholding Farmers	3.0	0.7	2.1	7.1	17.2	2.7	0.7	0.3	0.2	34.0
% of Cash Value	0.0	0.1	0.7	4.1	29.4	13.9	8.8	5.6	9.3	71.9
% of Non-Slaveholding Farmers	21.4	12.7	10.7	12.4	8.5	0.1	0.2	0.0	0.0	66.0
% of Cash Value	0.0	1.6	3.1	6.7	14.5	0.9	1.3	0.0	0.0	28.1

1860

% of Farm Population	22.1	6.2	10.1	14.5	34.0	5.4	5.3	2.2	0.2	100.0
% of Cash Value	0.0	0.4	1.3	3.6	25.4	12.6	26.7	24.2	5.8	100.0
% of Slaveholding Farmers	2.6	0.6	0.9	2.8	12.9	4.5	4.5	2.2	0.2	31.2
% of Cash Value	0.0	0.1	0.1	0.8	11.1	10.7	21.8	24.2	5.8	74.6
% of Non-Slaveholding Farmers	19.5	5.6	9.2	11.7	21.1	0.9	0.8	0.0	0.0	68.8
% of Cash Value	0.0	0.3	1.2	2.8	14.3	1.9	4.9	0.0	0.0	25.4

TABLE 79

DISTRIBUTION OF LIVESTOCK VALUE IN ANTEBELLUM TEXAS
REGION I (EAST TEXAS TIMBERLANDS), 1850 AND 1860

1850

$ Value of Livestock	0	1-99	100-249	250-499	500-999	1,000-1,499	1,500 1,999	2,000-4,999	5,000+	Totals
% of Farm Population	22.1	5.3	21.3	25.1	17.3	5.6	1.8	1.4	0.1	100.0
% of Livestock Value	0.0	0.8	9.2	22.6	30.1	17.0	7.9	11.0	1.4	100.0
% of Slaveholding Farmers	4.0	0.7	5.0	10.0	10.3	4.1	1.3	1.3	0.1	36.8
% of Livestock Value	0.0	0.1	2.3	9.3	18.4	12.2	5.8	9.8	1.4	59.3
% of Non-Slaveholding Farmers	18.1	4.6	16.3	15.1	7.0	1.5	0.5	0.1	0.0	63.2
% of Livestock Value	0.0	0.7	6.9	13.3	11.7	4.8	2.1	1.2	0.0	40.7

1860

% of Farm Population	16.1	1.8	14.2	23.4	23.5	8.9	4.8	6.2	1.1	100.0
% of Livestock Value	0.0	0.2	3.4	11.4	22.3	14.4	11.3	24.6	12.4	100.0
% of Slaveholding Farmers	1.6	0.1	1.4	6.7	12.6	6.1	3.9	4.7	1.0	38.1
% of Livestock Value	0.0	0.1	0.3	3.4	12.5	9.8	9.3	18.4	10.6	64.4
% of Non-Slaveholding Farmers	14.5	1.7	12.8	16.7	10.9	2.8	0.9	1.5	0.1	61.9
% of Livestock Value	0.0	0.1	3.1	8.0	9.8	4.6	2.0	6.2	1.8	35.6

TABLE 80

DISTRIBUTION OF LIVESTOCK VALUE IN ANTEBELLUM TEXAS
REGION II (GULF COASTAL PLAINS), 1850 AND 1860

1850

$ Value of Livestock	0	1-99	100-249	250-499	500-999	1,000-1,499	1,500-1,999	2,000-4,999	5,000+	Totals
% of Farm Population	19.7	3.8	10.9	12.7	19.7	10.0	5.3	12.9	5.0	100.0
% of Livestock Value	0.0	0.2	1.4	3.4	10.6	9.1	6.9	30.2	38.2	100.0
% of Slaveholding Farmers	2.1	0.6	1.5	5.9	10.9	6.2	2.9	12.1	4.1	46.3
% of Livestock Value	0.0	0.1	0.2	1.5	6.0	5.7	3.8	28.4	32.3	78.0
% of Non-Slaveholding Farmers	17.6	3.2	9.4	6.8	8.8	3.8	2.4	0.8	0.9	53.7
% of Livestock Value	0.0	0.1	1.2	1.9	4.6	3.4	3.1	1.8	5.9	22.0

1860

$ Value of Livestock	0	1-99	100-249	250-499	500-999	1,000-1,499	1,500-1,999	2,000-4,999	5,000+	Totals
% of Farm Population	12.7	0.0	3.4	14.1	18.1	14.8	4.7	21.5	10.7	100.0
% of Livestock Value	0.0	0.0	0.2	2.0	5.1	7.0	2.9	24.0	58.8	100.0
% of Slaveholding Farmers	4.0	0.0	0.0	4.0	7.4	10.8	4.0	17.5	8.0	55.7
% of Livestock Value	0.0	0.0	0.0	0.6	2.0	5.2	2.5	19.8	42.9	73.0
% of Non-Slaveholding Farmers	8.7	0.0	3.4	10.1	10.7	4.0	0.7	4.0	2.7	44.3
% of Livestock Value	0.0	0.0	0.2	1.4	3.1	1.8	0.4	4.2	15.9	27.0

TABLE 81

DISTRIBUTION OF LIVESTOCK VALUE IN ANTEBELLUM TEXAS
REGION III (NORTH-CENTRAL PRAIRIE), 1850 AND 1860

1850

$ Value of Livestock	0	1-99	100-249	250-499	500-999	1,000-1,499	1,500-1,999	2,000-4,999	5,000+	Totals
% of Farm Population	13.6	6.4	24.4	28.7	17.1	6.2	1.9	1.6	0.1	100.0
% of Livestock Value	0.0	1.0	10.2	23.9	28.1	17.6	7.6	9.6	2.0	100.0
% of Slaveholding Farmers	0.4	0.3	2.0	5.3	5.8	2.1	1.1	1.3	0.1	18.4
% of Livestock Value	0.0	0.1	0.9	4.6	9.9	6.1	4.4	8.2	2.0	36.2
% of Non-Slaveholding Farmers	13.2	6.1	22.4	23.4	11.3	4.1	0.8	0.3	0.0	81.6
% of Livestock Value	0.0	0.9	9.3	19.3	18.2	11.5	3.2	1.4	0.0	63.8

1860

$ Value of Livestock	0	1-99	100-249	250-499	500-999	1,000-1,499	1,500-1,999	2,000-4,999	5,000+	Totals
% of Farm Population	26.6	1.6	7.3	14.2	20.9	10.7	7.0	9.8	1.9	100.0
% of Livestock Value	0.0	0.1	1.3	5.3	15.6	13.1	12.5	30.0	22.1	100.0
% of Slaveholding Farmers	1.8	0.1	0.6	1.8	4.7	3.8	2.1	5.8	1.5	22.2
% of Livestock Value	0.0	0.0	0.1	0.7	3.7	4.7	3.7	18.2	17.6	48.7
% of Non-Slaveholding Farmers	24.8	1.5	6.7	12.4	16.2	6.9	4.9	4.0	0.4	77.8
% of Livestock Value	0.0	0.1	1.2	4.6	11.9	8.4	8.8	11.8	4.5	51.3

TABLE 82

DISTRIBUTION OF LIVESTOCK VALUE IN ANTEBELLUM TEXAS
REGION IV (SOUTH-CENTRAL AREA), 1850 AND 1860

1850

$ Value of Livestock	0	1-99	100-249	250-499	500-999	1,000-1,499	1,500-1,999	2,000-4,999	5,000+	Totals
% of Farm Population	17.3	2.1	19.3	17.1	22.8	9.6	4.4	5.8	1.6	100.0
% of Livestock Value	0.0	0.2	4.6	8.8	21.6	15.6	10.5	23.1	15.6	100.0
% of Slaveholding Farmers	1.6	0.3	2.2	4.5	10.3	6.6	2.8	4.3	1.5	34.1
% of Livestock Value	0.0	0.1	0.6	2.4	10.3	10.6	6.7	17.4	14.3	62.4
% of Non-Slaveholding Farmers	15.7	1.8	17.1	12.6	12.5	3.0	1.6	1.5	0.1	65.9
% of Livestock Value	0.0	0.1	4.0	6.4	11.3	5.0	3.8	5.7	1.3	37.6

1860

$ Value of Livestock	0	1-99	100-249	250-499	500-999	1,000-1,499	1,500-1,999	2,000-4,999	5,000+	Totals
% of Farm Population	19.4	1.3	9.7	17.9	16.8	10.3	5.7	13.9	5.0	100.0
% of Livestock Value	0.0	0.1	1.3	5.0	9.0	9.5	7.6	32.5	35.0	100.0
% of Slaveholding Farmers	1.9	0.0	0.5	2.7	4.1	5.2	3.1	9.5	4.1	31.1
% of Livestock Value	0.0	0.0	0.1	0.7	2.2	4.8	4.0	22.3	28.7	62.8
% of Non-Slaveholding Farmers	17.5	1.3	9.2	15.2	12.7	5.1	2.6	4.4	0.9	68.7
% of Livestock Value	0.0	0.1	1.2	4.3	6.8	4.7	3.6	10.2	6.3	37.2

TABLE 83

DISTRIBUTION OF CORN PRODUCTION IN ANTEBELLUM TEXAS
REGION I (EAST TEXAS TIMBERLANDS), 1850 AND 1860

1850

Bushels of Corn	0	1-99	100-249	250-499	500-999	1,000-1,499	1,500-1,999	2,000-4,999	5,000+	Totals
% of Farm Population	30.6	6.0	25.3	18.5	12.4	4.2	1.3	1.6	0.1	100.0
% of Corn Crop	0.0	1.1	13.4	21.0	26.7	15.5	6.7	12.7	2.9	100.0
% of Slaveholding Farmers	7.0	1.4	6.2	7.4	8.2	3.6	1.2	1.6	0.1	36.7
% of Corn Crop	0.0	0.3	3.4	8.8	17.7	13.1	6.5	12.7	2.9	65.4
% of Non-Slaveholding Farmers	23.6	4.6	19.1	11.1	4.2	0.6	0.1	0.0	0.0	63.3
% of Corn Crop	0.0	0.8	10.1	12.2	9.0	2.4	0.2	0.0	0.0	34.6

1860

Bushels of Corn	0	1-99	100-249	250-499	500-999	1,000-1,499	1,500-1,999	2,000-4,999	5,000+	Totals
% of Farm Population	20.3	3.7	26.6	22.6	15.9	4.8	2.8	2.7	0.6	100.0
% of Corn Crop	0.0	0.5	9.8	17.6	23.7	12.6	10.4	16.6	8.8	100.0
% of Slaveholding Farmers	3.1	0.5	4.9	8.1	10.9	4.4	2.8	2.7	0.6	38.0
% of Corn Crop	0.0	0.1	1.9	6.7	16.8	11.6	10.4	16.6	8.8	72.9
% of Non-Slaveholding Farmers	17.2	3.2	21.7	14.5	5.0	0.4	0.0	0.0	0.0	62.0
% of Corn Crop	0.0	0.4	7.9	10.9	6.9	1.0	0.0	0.0	0.0	27.1

TABLE 84

DISTRIBUTION OF CORN PRODUCTION IN ANTEBELLUM TEXAS
REGION II (GULF COASTAL PLAINS), 1850 AND 1860

1850

Bushels of Corn	0	1-99	100-249	250-499	500-999	1,000-1,499	1,500-1,999	2,000-4,999	5,000+	Totals
% of Farm Population	32.6	10.0	20.3	12.4	10.0	3.5	1.8	7.6	1.8	100.0
% of Corn Crop	0.0	1.0	5.2	7.7	11.7	7.2	5.1	38.8	23.3	100.0
% of Slaveholding Farmers	8.2	1.2	6.5	8.6	7.4	3.2	1.8	7.6	1.8	46.3
% of Corn Crop	0.0	0.1	1.8	5.4	8.7	6.7	5.1	38.8	23.3	89.9
% of Non-Slaveholding Farmers	24.4	8.8	13.8	3.8	2.6	0.3	0.0	0.0	0.0	53.7
% of Corn Crop	0.0	0.0	3.4	2.3	3.0	0.5	0.0	0.0	0.0	10.1

1860

Bushels of Corn	0	1-99	100-249	250-499	500-999	1,000-1,499	1,500-1,999	2,000-4,999	5,000+	Totals
% of Farm Population	21.5	4.7	18.1	14.1	15.4	11.4	2.0	8.1	4.7	100.0
% of Corn Crop	0.0	0.3	2.8	4.7	10.7	12.7	3.3	22.5	43.0	100.0
% of Slaveholding Farmers	6.1	1.3	5.4	6.7	11.4	10.1	2.0	8.1	4.7	55.8
% of Corn Crop	0.0	0.1	0.9	2.4	8.1	11.1	3.3	22.5	43.0	91.4
% of Non-Slaveholding Farmers	15.4	3.4	12.7	7.4	4.0	1.3	0.0	0.0	0.0	44.2
% of Corn Crop	0.0	0.2	1.9	2.3	2.6	1.6	0.0	0.0	0.0	8.6

TABLE 85

DISTRIBUTION OF CORN PRODUCTION IN ANTEBELLUM TEXAS
REGION III (NORTH-CENTRAL PRAIRIES), 1850 AND 1860

1850

Bushels of Corn	0	1-99	100-249	250-499	500-999	1,000-1,499	1,500-1,999	2,000-4,999	5,000+	Totals
% of Farm Population	31.7	8.2	25.3	19.7	10.9	2.9	0.3	0.8	0.2	100.0
% of Corn Crop	0.0	1.6	16.6	26.4	27.5	12.2	1.6	7.4	6.6	100.0
% of Slaveholding Farmers	3.6	1.4	3.2	4.1	3.3	1.7	0.3	0.7	0.1	18.4
% of Corn Crop	0.0	0.3	2.0	5.6	8.6	7.2	1.6	6.0	3.3	34.6
% of Non-Slaveholding Farmers	28.1	6.8	22.1	15.6	7.6	1.2	0.0	0.1	0.1	81.6
% of Corn Crop	0.0	1.3	14.6	20.8	19.0	5.0	0.0	1.4	3.3	65.4

1860

Bushels of Corn	0	1-99	100-249	250-499	500-999	1,000-1,499	1,500-1,999	2,000-4,999	5,000+	Totals
% of Farm Population	40.2	11.7	22.9	14.1	6.7	2.3	1.0	1.0	0.1	100.0
% of Corn Crop	0.0	3.1	17.3	23.7	20.9	13.1	7.7	11.9	2.3	100.0
% of Slaveholding Farmers	4.5	1.6	4.0	4.8	3.9	1.6	0.9	0.9	0.1	22.3
% of Corn Crop	0.0	0.4	3.4	8.7	11.9	9.1	7.0	11.0	2.3	53.8
% of Non-Slaveholding Farmers	35.7	10.1	18.9	9.3	2.8	0.7	0.1	0.1	0.0	77.7
% of Corn Crop	0.0	2.7	13.9	15.0	9.0	4.0	0.7	0.9	0.0	46.2

TABLE 86

DISTRIBUTION OF CORN PRODUCTION IN ANTEBELLUM TEXAS
REGION IV (SOUTH-CENTRAL AREA), 1850 AND 1860

1850

Bushels of Corn	0	1-99	100-249	250-499	500-999	1,000-1,499	1,500-1,999	2,000-4,999	5,000+	Totals
% of Farm Population	25.3	5.6	21.8	19.1	16.5	6.0	2.1	3.3	0.3	100.0
% of Corn Crop	0.0	0.8	8.7	16.3	26.3	16.4	8.3	19.4	3.8	100.0
% of Slaveholding Farmers	3.0	0.7	4.0	6.3	10.1	4.9	2.1	2.7	0.3	34.1
% of Corn Crop	0.0	0.1	1.7	5.3	17.1	13.6	8.3	16.2	3.8	66.1
% of Non-Slaveholding Farmers	22.3	4.9	17.8	12.8	6.4	1.1	0.0	0.6	0.0	65.9
% of Corn Crop	0.0	0.7	7.0	11.0	9.2	2.8	0.0	3.2	0.0	33.9

1860

Bushels of Corn	0	1-99	100-249	250-499	500-999	1,000-1,499	1,500-1,999	2,000-4,999	5,000+	Totals
% of Farm Population	35.9	15.7	22.1	11.9	6.3	2.8	2.4	2.8	0.1	100.0
% of Corn Crop	0.0	2.5	12.6	14.9	15.1	11.6	14.1	26.4	2.8	100.0
% of Slaveholding Farmers	5.2	2.1	6.8	5.0	4.3	2.6	2.4	2.7	0.1	31.2
% of Corn Crop	0.0	0.4	4.0	6.5	10.4	10.6	14.1	25.2	2.8	74.0
% of Non-Slaveholding Farmers	30.7	13.6	15.3	6.9	2.0	0.2	0.0	0.1	0.0	68.8
% of Corn Crop	0.0	2.1	8.6	8.4	4.7	1.0	0.0	1.2	0.0	26.0

TABLE 87

DISTRIBUTION OF COTTON PRODUCTION IN ANTEBELLUM TEXAS
REGION I (EAST TEXAS TIMBERLANDS), 1850 AND 1860

1850

Bales of Cotton	0	1-4	5-9	10-19	20-49	50-99	100-149	150-199	200+	Totals
% of Farm Population	69.1	16.9	7.6	2.7	3.0	0.6	0.1	0.0	0.0	100.0
% of Cotton Crop	0.0	14.8	19.3	14.1	33.1	16.7	2.0	0.0	0.0	100.0
% of Slaveholding Farmers	18.1	6.7	5.7	2.5	3.0	0.6	0.1	0.0	0.0	36.7
% of Cotton Crop	0.0	6.6	14.7	13.2	33.1	16.7	2.0	0.0	0.0	86.3
% of Non-Slaveholding Farmers	51.0	10.2	1.9	0.2	0.0	0.0	0.0	0.0	0.0	63.3
% of Cotton Crop	0.0	8.2	4.6	0.9	0.0	0.0	0.0	0.0	0.0	13.7

1860

Bales of Cotton	0	1-4	5-9	10-19	20-49	50-99	100-149	150-199	200+	Totals
% of Farm Population	41.8	23.3	12.4	9.3	7.6	3.8	0.8	0.4	0.6	100.0
% of Cotton Crop	0.0	4.9	7.3	11.1	21.6	24.3	8.8	5.7	16.3	100.0
% of Slaveholding Farmers	7.8	3.7	5.7	7.8	7.4	3.8	0.8	0.4	0.6	38.0
% of Cotton Crop	0.0	0.9	3.6	9.4	21.2	24.3	8.8	5.7	16.3	90.2
% of Non-Slaveholding Farmers	34.0	19.6	6.7	1.5	0.2	0.0	0.0	0.0	0.0	62.0
% of Cotton Crop	0.0	4.0	3.7	1.7	0.4	0.0	0.0	0.0	0.0	9.8

TABLE 88

DISTRIBUTION OF COTTON PRODUCTION IN ANTEBELLUM TEXAS
REGION II (GULF COASTAL PLAINS), 1850 AND 1860

1850

Bales of Cotton	0	1-4	5-9	10-19	20-49	50-99	100-149	150-199	200+	Totals
% of Farm Population	83.8	3.2	1.8	2.4	3.5	3.5	1.2	0.3	0.3	100.0
% of Cotton Crop	0.0	1.4	2.1	4.3	17.1	33.1	20.4	6.9	14.7	100.0
% of Slaveholding Farmers	31.2	2.3	1.5	2.4	3.5	3.5	1.2	0.3	0.3	46.2
% of Cotton Crop	0.0	1.2	1.7	4.3	17.1	33.1	20.4	6.9	14.7	99.4
% of Non-Slaveholding Farmers	52.6	0.9	0.3	0.0	0.0	0.0	0.0	0.0	0.0	53.8
% of Cotton Crop	0.0	0.2	0.4	0.0	0.0	0.0	0.0	0.0	0.0	0.6

1860

Bales of Cotton	0	1-4	5-9	10-19	20-49	50-99	100-149	150-199	200+	Totals
% of Farm Population	61.7	4.7	3.4	4.7	11.4	4.7	4.0	1.4	4.0	100.0
% of Cotton Crop	0.0	0.3	0.7	2.3	11.0	9.5	14.6	7.1	54.5	100.0
% of Slaveholding Farmers	24.1	1.3	1.4	3.4	11.4	4.7	4.0	1.4	4.0	55.7
% of Cotton Crop	0.0	0.1	0.3	1.7	11.0	9.5	14.6	7.1	54.5	98.8
% of Non-Slaveholding Farmers	37.6	3.4	2.0	1.3	0.0	0.0	0.0	0.0	0.0	44.3
% of Cotton Crop	0.0	0.2	0.4	0.6	0.0	0.0	0.0	0.0	0.0	1.2

TABLE 89

DISTRIBUTION OF COTTON PRODUCTION IN ANTEBELLUM TEXAS
REGION III (NORTH-CENTRAL PRAIRIE), 1850 AND 1860

1850

Bales of Cotton	0	1-4	5-9	10-19	20-49	50-99	100-149	150-199	200+	Totals
% of Farm Population	91.1	6.5	1.6	0.3	0.5	0.0	0.0	0.0	0.0	100.0
% of Cotton Crop	0.0	30.4	21.9	6.9	40.8	0.0	0.0	0.0	0.0	100.0
% of Slaveholding Farmers	14.6	2.5	0.5	0.3	0.5	0.0	0.0	0.0	0.0	18.4
% of Cotton Crop	0.0	15.4	7.2	6.9	40.8	0.0	0.0	0.0	0.0	70.3
% of Non-Slaveholding Farmers	76.5	4.0	1.1	0.0	0.0	0.0	0.0	0.0	0.0	81.6
% of Cotton Crop	0.0	15.0	14.7	0.0	0.0	0.0	0.0	0.0	0.0	29.7

1860

Bales of Cotton	0	1-4	5-9	10-19	20-49	50-99	100-149	150-199	200+	Totals
% of Farm Population	92.0	3.1	2.0	1.6	0.8	0.3	0.1	0.1	0.0	100.0
% of Cotton Crop	0.0	7.1	11.9	19.5	23.4	14.6	8.3	15.2	0.0	100.0
% of Slaveholding Farmers	16.6	1.8	1.3	1.2	0.8	0.3	0.1	0.1	0.0	22.2
% of Cotton Crop	0.0	4.1	7.5	15.3	23.4	14.6	8.3	15.2	0.0	88.4
% of Non-Slaveholding Farmers	75.4	1.3	0.7	0.4	0.0	0.0	0.0	0.0	0.0	77.8
% of Cotton Crop	0.0	3.0	4.4	4.2	0.0	0.0	0.0	0.0	0.0	11.6

TABLE 90

DISTRIBUTION OF COTTON PRODUCTION IN ANTEBELLUM TEXAS
REGION IV (SOUTH-CENTRAL AREA), 1850 AND 1860

1850

Bales of Cotton	0	1-4	5-9	10-19	20-49	50-99	100-149	150-199	200+	Totals
% of Farm Population	73.4	10.3	5.3	5.4	4.3	1.3	0.0	0.0	0.0	100.0
% of Cotton Crop	0.0	7.5	9.9	19.0	40.8	22.8	0.0	0.0	0.0	100.0
% of Slaveholding Farmers	18.3	3.3	2.5	4.3	4.3	1.3	0.0	0.0	0.0	34.0
% of Cotton Crop	0.0	2.7	4.6	15.7	40.8	22.8	0.0	0.0	0.0	86.6
% of Non-Slaveholding Farmers	55.1	7.0	2.8	1.1	0.0	0.0	0.0	0.0	0.0	66.0
% of Cotton Crop	0.0	4.8	5.3	3.3	0.0	0.0	0.0	0.0	0.0	13.4

1860

Bales of Cotton	0	1-4	5-9	10-19	20-49	50-99	100-149	150-199	200+	Totals
% of Farm Population	53.6	17.0	10.8	8.0	5.1	3.2	1.3	0.5	0.5	100.0
% of Cotton Crop	0.0	3.9	7.5	11.2	15.7	22.9	16.6	9.1	13.1	100.0
% of Slaveholding Farmers	10.0	2.9	3.2	4.9	4.7	3.2	1.3	0.5	0.5	31.2
% of Cotton Crop	0.0	0.8	2.4	7.1	14.5	22.9	16.6	9.1	13.1	86.5
% of Non-Slaveholding Farmers	43.6	14.1	7.6	3.1	0.4	0.0	0.0	0.0	0.0	68.8
% of Cotton Crop	0.0	3.1	5.1	4.1	1.2	0.0	0.0	0.0	0.0	13.5

Bibliography

Manuscripts

Records of the Comptroller of Public Accounts, Ad Valorem Tax Division. County Real and Personal Property Tax Rolls, 1836-1874. Archives Division, Texas State Library, Austin.

Records of the Secretary of State. Election Registers, 1846-1854 and 1854-1861. Archives Division, Texas State Library, Austin.

Seventh Census of the United States, 1850. Schedules I (Free Inhabitants), II (Slave Inhabitants), and IV (Productions of Agriculture). Schedules I and II are housed in the National Archives, Washington, D.C. Schedule IV is in the Archives Division, Texas State Library, Austin.

Eighth Census of the United States, 1860. Schedules I (Free Inhabitants), II (Slave Inhabitants), and IV (Productions of Agriculture). Schedules I and II are housed in the National Archives, Washington, D.C. Schedule IV is in the Archives Division, Texas State Library, Austin.

Published Documents, Federal and State

Biographical Directory of the American Congress, 1774-1949. Washington, D.C.: Government Printing Office, 1950.

DeBow, J. D. B., ed. *Statistical View of the United States . . . Being a Compendium of the Seventh Census . . .* Washington, D.C.: Beverley Tucker, Senate Printer, 1854.

Members of The Texas Legislature, 1846-1962. Austin: Texas State Legislature, 1962.

Texas Agricultural Experiment Station, Texas A&M University. "The General Soil Map of Texas." College Station: Texas A&M University, 1973.

United States. Bureau of the Census. *Eighth Census of the United States*. 4 vols. Washington, D.C.: Government Printing Office, 1864.

Wallace, Ernest, and David M. Vigness, eds. *Documents of Texas History*. Austin: Steck Company, 1963.

Winkler, Ernest William, ed. *Platforms of Political Parties in Texas*. Austin: The University of Texas, 1916.

Books

Cairnes, John E. *The Slave Power: Its Character, Career, and Probable Designs,*

Being an Attempt To Explain the Real Issues Involved in the American Contest. London: Macmillan, 1863. 2nd edition.

Clark, Blanche H. *The Tennessee Yeoman, 1840-1860.* Nashville: Vanderbilt University Press, 1942.

Connor, Seymour V. *Texas, A History.* New York: Thomas Y. Crowell Company, 1971.

Dollar, Charles M., and Richard J. Jensen. *Historian's Guide to Statistics: Quantitative Analysis and Historical Research.* New York: Holt, Rinehart and Winston, 1971.

Dyer, Gustavus W. *Democracy in the South before the Civil War.* Nashville and Dallas: Publishing House of the Methodist Episcopal Church, South, 1905.

Fogel, Robert W., and Stanley L. Engerman. *Time on the Cross: The Economics of American Negro Slavery.* 2 vols. Boston: Little, Brown, 1974.

Genovese, Eugene D. *The Political Economy of Slavery: Studies in the Economy and Society of the Slave South.* New York: Pantheon Books, 1965.

Gray, Lewis Cecil. *History of Agriculture in the Southern United States to 1860.* 2 vols. Washington, D.C.: Carnegie Institution of Washington, 1933.

Howe, John R. *From the Revolution through the Age of Jackson: Innocence and Empire in the Young Republic.* Englewood Cliffs, New Jersey: Prentice-Hall, 1973.

Hogan, William R. *The Texas Republic: A Social and Economic History.* Norman: University of Oklahoma Press, 1946.

Lampman, Robert J. *The Share of Top Wealth-holders in National Wealth, 1922-1956.* Princeton, New Jersey: Princeton University Press, 1962.

Lathrop, Barnes F. *Migration into East Texas, 1850-1860: A Study from the United States Census.* Austin: Texas State Historical Association, 1949.

Litwack, Leon F. *North of Slavery: The Negro in the Free States, 1790-1860.* Chicago, Illinois: University of Chicago Press, 1961.

Meinig, Donald W. *Imperial Texas: An Interpretive Essay in Cultural Geography.* Austin: University of Texas Press, 1969.

Olmsted, Frederick Law. *A Journey in the Back Country.* New York: Mason Brothers, 1860.

———. *A Journey in the Seaboard Slave States, with Remarks on Their Economy.* New York: Dix & Edwards, 1856.

———. *A Journey through Texas: or, A Saddle-Trip on the Southwestern Frontier, with a Statistical Appendix.* New York: Dix, Edwards & Company, 1857.

Owsley, Frank Lawrence. *Plain Folk of the Old South.* Baton Rouge: Louisiana State University Press, 1949.

Pessen, Edward. *Riches, Class, and Power before the Civil War.* Lexington, Massachusetts: D. C. Heath, 1973.

Phillips, Ulrich B. *American Negro Slavery: A Survey of the Supply, Employment, and Control of Negro Labor as Determined by the Plantation Regime.* New York: D. Appleton and Company, 1918.

———. *Life and Labor in the Old South.* Boston: Little, Brown, and Company, 1929.

Projector, Dorothy S., and Gertrude S. Weiss, eds. *Survey of Financial Characteristics of Consumers.* Washington, D.C.: Federal Reserve System Technical Papers, 1966.

Rhodes, James Ford. *History of The United States from the Compromise of 1850 to . . . 1877.* 7 vols. New York: Macmillan, 1893-1906.

Richardson, Rupert N., Ernest Wallace, and Adrian Anderson. *Texas: The Lone Star State.* Englewood Cliffs, New Jersey: Prentice-Hall, 1970. 3rd edition.

Soltow, Lee. *Men and Wealth in the United States, 1850-1870.* New Haven and London: Yale University Press, 1975.

———. *Patterns of Wealthholding in Wisconsin since 1850.* Madison: University of Wisconsin Press, 1971.

The Texas Almanac and State Industrial Guide, 1970-1971. Dallas, Texas: A. H. Belo Corporation, 1969.

Weaver, Herbert. *Mississippi Farmers, 1850-1860.* Nashville: Vanderbilt University Press, 1945.

Webb, Walter Prescott et al., eds. *The Handbook of Texas.* 2 vols. Austin: Texas State Historical Association, 1952.

Wheeler, Kenneth W. *To Wear a City's Crown: The Beginnings of Urban Growth in Texas, 1836-1865.* Cambridge, Massachusetts: Harvard University Press, 1968.

Wooster, Ralph A. *The People in Power: Courthouse and Statehouse in the Lower South, 1850-1860.* Knoxville: University of Tennessee Press, 1969.

Wright, Carroll D. *The History and Growth of the United States Census.* Washington, D.C.: United States Government Printing Office, 1900.

Articles

Blumin, Stuart. "Mobility and Change in Ante-Bellum Philadelphia." In Stephan Thernstrom and Richard Sennett, eds., *Nineteenth-Century Cities: Essays in the New Urban History,* pp. 165-208. New Haven, Connecticut: Yale University Press, 1969.

Campbell, Randolph. "Local Archives as a Source of Slave Prices: Harrison County, Texas, as a Test Case." *The Historian* 36 (August, 1974), 660-670.

Evans, Robert, Jr. "The Economics of American Negro Slavery." In *Aspects of Labor Economics, A Conference of the Universities-National Bureau Committee for Economic Research*, pp. 185-243. Princeton: Princeton University Press, 1962.

Gallman, Robert E. "Trends in the Size Distribution of Wealth in the Nineteenth Century: Some Speculations." In Lee Soltow, ed., *Six Papers on the Size Distribution of Wealth and Income*, vol. 33 of *Studies in Income and Wealth*, pp. 1-30. New York: National Bureau of Economic Research, 1969.

Green, Fletcher M. "Democracy in the Old South." *Journal of Southern History* 12 (February, 1946), 3-23.

King, Willford I. "Wealth Distribution in the Continental United States at the Close of 1921." *Journal of the American Statistical Association* 22 (June, 1927), 135-153.

Linden, Fabian. "Economic Democracy in the Slave South: An Appraisal of Some Recent Views." *Journal of Negro History* 31 (April, 1946), 140-190.

Lorenz, M. O. "Methods of Measuring the Concentration of Wealth." *Publications of the American Statistical Association* 9 (June, 1905), 209-219.

Middleton, Annie. "The Texas Convention of 1845." *Southwestern Historical Quarterly* 25 (July, 1921), 26-62.

Owsley, Frank L. "Communications to the Editor." *American Historical Review* 52 (July, 1947), 845-849.

———, and Harriet C. Owsley. "The Economic Basis of Society in the Late Ante-Bellum South." *Journal of Southern History* 6 (February, 1940), 24-45.

Paxson, Frederic L. "The Constitution of Texas, 1845." *Southwestern Historical Quarterly* 18 (April, 1915), 386-398.

Phillips, Ulrich B. "The Origin and Growth of the Southern Black Belts." *American Historical Review* 11 (July, 1906), 798-816.

Potter, David M. "Depletion and Renewal in Southern History." In Edgar T. Thompson, ed. *Perspectives on the South: Agenda for Research*, pp. 75-89. Durham, North Carolina: Duke University Press, 1967.

Rothstein, Morton. "The Cotton Frontier of the Antebellum United States: A Methodological Battleground." *Agricultural History* 44 (January, 1970), 149-165.

Wooster, Ralph A. "An Analysis of the Membership of the Texas Secession Convention." *Southwestern Historical Quarterly* 62 (January, 1959), 328-335.

———. "Foreigners in the Principal Towns of Ante-Bellum Texas." *Southwestern Historical Quarterly* 66 (October, 1962), 208-220.

Wright, Gavin. " 'Economic Democracy' and the Concentration of Agricultural Wealth in the Cotton South, 1850-1860." *Agricultural History* 44 (January, 1970), 63-93.

Index

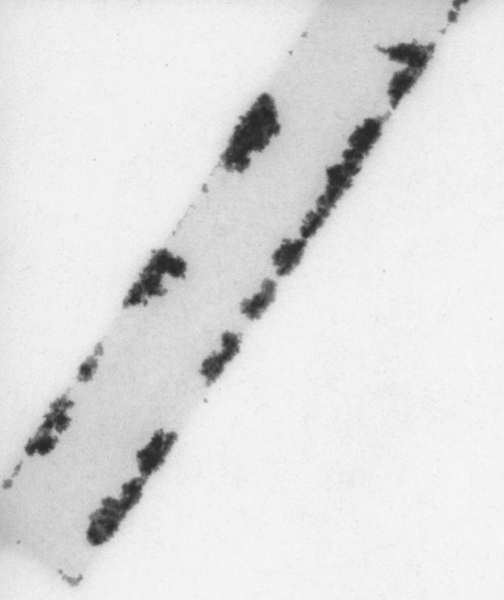